Om, baby!
a pilgrimage to the eternal self

Jack Haas

Copyright© 2005 Jack Haas

All rights reserved. No part of this publication may be reproduced or transmitted in any form or by any means, electronic or mechanical, including photocopying, recording, or by any information storage or retrieval system, without written permission from the Publisher, except in quoting brief passages.

Thanks to Maggie McGhee and Tanis Mager for their valuable editing skills.

Library and Archives Canada Cataloguing in Publication

Haas, Jack, 1966-
    Om, baby! : a pilgrimage to the eternal self / Jack Haas.

Includes bibliographical references.
ISBN 0-9734677-1-1

1. Haas, Jack, 1966- 2. Spiritual biography. I. Title.

PS8565.A145Z473 2005   200'.92   C2005-901201-3

Published by Iconoclast Press:
Suite 144
3495 Cambie St.
Vancouver, BC.
V5Z 4R3
Canada

email: admin@iconoclastpress.com

About the front cover: the picture is a blending of one of my paintings, and a photograph of me taken in India. The juxtaposition represents the union of my invisible, infinite female self, with my visible, finite, male form- that is, the union of my macrocosmic and microcosmic self.

To the living spirit of Jesus, the Christ.
Alive and well, strong and resolute, loving and defiant.
I salute you.

"My faith is the greatest of faiths and the least of faiths,
Enclosing worship ancient and modern and all between ancient and modern,
Believing I shall come again upon the earth after five thousand years,
Waiting responses from oracles, honoring the gods, saluting the sun,
Making a fetish of the first rock or stump, powowing with sticks in the circle of obis,
Helping the llama or brahmin as he trims the lamps of the idols,
Dancing yet through the streets in a phallic procession, rapt and austere in the woods a gymnosophist,
Drinking mead from the skull-cap, to Shastas and Vedas admirant, minding the Koran,
Walking the teokallis, spotted with gore from the stone and knife, beating the serpent-skin drum,
Accepting the Gospels, accepting him that was crucified, knowing assuredly that he is divine,
To the mass kneeling or the puritan's prayer rising, or sitting patiently in a pew,
Ranting and frothing in my insane crisis, or waiting dead-like till my spirit arouses me,
Looking forth on pavement and land, or outside of pavement and land,
Belonging to the winders of the circuit of circuits.

One of that centripetal and centrifugal gang I turn and talk like a man leaving charges before a journey.

I too am not a bit tamed, I too am untranslatable,
I sound my barbaric yawp over the roofs of the world...

I bequeath myself to the dirt to grow from the grass I love,
If you want me again look for me under your boot-soles.

You will hardly know who I am or what I mean,
But I shall be good health to you nevertheless,
And filter and fibre your blood.

Failing to fetch me at first keep encouraged,
Missing me one place search another,
I stop somewhere waiting for you."
    Walt Whitman

THE TREE OF LIFE
mandala by the author

Part I
TRANSFORMATION

"Come to the edge," he said.
They said, "We are afraid."
"Come to the edge," he said.
They came, he pushed them...
And they flew.
Appolinaire

chapter one

There is no man or woman who walks upon this crazy earth who is not a privileged pilgrim on a fantastic journey to the temple of their own immortal soul. There is no life cast upon the wild shores of this mysterious world which does not belong intimately to the fabric and fantasy sewn inexorably into the all. There is no separate individual who is not therefore part and parcel with the whole. For the all is without division, without futility, and within us all. We are the all that is the all. There is nothing but the everything that we are. For we are one. Amen.

Our journey takes us from our personal myth and mystery, on to the Great Myth and Great Mystery. Our path leads from our separate body to the One Great Body.

It is a hallowed and never ending journey to this oneness that ends as it began- in confusion; a confusion which is both the substratum of life and the very goal of life which has no end. For a goal which can be completed is of little value to the eternal Self.

In this way existence is quite like a fractal; the more we go into it, the more it expands, the more patterns emerge from within other patterns, universes emerge from the smallest iota, solving one problem often creates many others, coming to one realization uncovers multiple enigmas, attaining one peak reveals a higher mountain range behind it, and the threads of the overself paradoxically cover and yet also reveal the limitlessness of the magnificent cosmic carpet running out ineffably before us.

Nothing ever finishes. Impermanence is everlasting. Through the temporal we find the eternal, and through the eternal we find the now.

The journey never ends, it merely changes direction. Eternity spills into us from without, and pours out of us from within, and we are the open, ephemeral gate through which the divided waters of heaven and earth mix into the roaring confluence of immortal streams. And yet we are the calm depths beneath the crashing surf as well. We are the stillness behind the fabulous change.

Life is thus an ongoing banquet of possibilities, implausibilities, challenges, miracles, boredom, distress, lunacy, euphoria, awe, and affirmations. And the show will go on and on and on, and until an individual realizes this predicament of eternity, he or she will continue to pursue a goal whose reward is only another challenge, which is why it is important to love your soul, because nothing suffers more from a lie than the soul. And the immortal soul, trapped within the ephemeral show, will suffer from the lie of time worst of all.

I should know, for I have drunk the blood of woundedness and loss, and I have raged against the folly of our incorrigible predicament. And I have gnashed and wailed before the portal of infinity. But I have done this because of growing pains I did not know were there, for I had covered them over with the illusion of tomorrow; I had entertained the idea that there was a splendid reward waiting somewhere in the future. But then I realized that there was no such thing as a future except within the lie of time; outside of time there is only eternity, which is what we call *now*. And so *now* it is my time to shout the roar of immortal glory, instead of wailing the tears of time. It is now my non-time to rip the world open with a mind that cannot understand what comes through it to rip the world open. This is the mystery of now. This is my inspiration.

It is my inspiration because I have dwelled within the paradigm of time and of our erroneous separation for a lengthy duration, but while drowning in the depths of such an ensconcing sea I unexpectedly found that I had learned to breathe under water. Which is to say, I had discovered inspiration.

I know now that all of my compulsions have been the outcome of my primary addiction- the need for inspiration. Inspiration is my drug. Such things as spirituality, booze, travel, psychedelics, contemplation, music, dance, laughter, wilderness, and ribaldry- these have simply been the different forms of the drug of inspiration for which I have had great need in this confounding life. I could not live without being inspired, be it from beauty, wonder, intoxication, love, God, adventure, merriment, or profundity. And that means I have been an addict to perhaps the most relentless addiction of them all, because any moment I was not soaking in the thick tremor of inspiration was but an agony waiting to be relieved. And relieve it I did.

Oh, did I relieve it. I went mad with anguish and euphoria. I tramped and wandered and roamed this magnificent earth. I drank and smoked and ingested the bounty of the earth's intoxicants. I studied and scoured and devoured this inexorable mystery into which I was born. I laughed and wept and played and roared at the glory and gore of this whole mad show. I walked away and came back again. I ran away and returned. I shouted with rage and bellowed with praise. I fought with fists and made love with wild abandon. I sought inspiration in the guts, the heart, the spirit, and in the bowels of our cosmic corpulescence. And whether it was right or wrong no longer matters, for I could have done no other. I could not live without inspiration. I knew this, and I resigned. Inspiration would be my oxygen.

And yet all the jangle and boom which resounded from my feverish endeavors were themselves but aspects of only one half of my true nature. The other half was stillness. Absolute stillness. And it was not until that stillness devoid of opposites arose within me did I truly realize my inexorable addiction. It was not until I blew apart in a subtle super-nova caused by the coalescence of all I had endured, that I then merged into the all from which I had been sucking inspiration.

It was from this apocalyptic transformation that I became still. But even as the peace and equanimity of the limitless void dissolved and became me, and I became that oxygen I once so feverishly inhaled, still did I look out from the eternal harbor of the eternal self. And with a subtle grin of excitement I learned to settle comfortably back into the flesh, knowing that no word describes this inspired life of action and peace better than *Hallelujah*!

Passion and dispassion now merge within me as if I am at rest amidst an apocalypse. I am at the still point, and I am in the maelstrom. I am calm, and I am exploding. I am full of faith, and I am wild with mania. I am love, and I am rage.

I am a rock rising inviolably out of the sea, and I am the roaring waves trying to break it.

I am the horror and the caress, the thrashing and the quiescence, the pandemonium and the peace.

I am the link between the one and the many, the perfection and the dross, the glory and the gore, the victory and the loss.

I am an invisible bridge between invisible worlds, a tightrope uniting spirit and flesh, heaven and earth, ennui and ecstasy, becoming and eternity. There is no end. And I am no longer afraid.

I am no longer afraid because I know *now* that fear is the wall which divides the ecstatic-All into agonizing parts. To take down the wall is to become the All. To become the All is to be torn into pieces like Osiris, only to then be re-membered into the eternal, divisionless realm of Love.

I am no longer afraid. And it is for this inextinguishable reason that like a madman with an unquenchable song in his tremulous heart do I now sing without shame for the glory. *Om, baby!*

*

two

Though words such as these are mere blind tremblings shouted into the distance as an admittance of impossible clarity, I nevertheless seek in my own imperfect way to share my journey without intending to create a map for others to follow. For there is no map, there is only a journey, a terrible and brilliant sojourn through the inexplicable flesh.

It is a journey fraught with confusion and fusion, an unavoidable undertaking beyond all comprehension and coherence.

It is a journey without certainty or plan. And yet the soul somehow knows its own way, if only one learns to trust and follow. To follow the soul is to realize that there is naught but a single question which looms at all crossroads, and that is- "Which way leads towards my greater perfection." There is no choice nor deliberation in the dark and confusing path of life, there is merely an ultimatum. For when the soul which knows the way lays down the gauntlet and points towards the dark abyss towards which we must wander, the only decision which remains is whether we begin our inner voyage now or later, for inevitably it is thither we must go.

We must go, so that we may then return.

And so, like the pendulous cosmogenesis of a lesser Brahma- who, it is said, exhales the universe for thousands of years, and then inhales it again until it dissolves back into Himself where it enters into the primal, unqualified state thousands of years later- did I inhale and absorb the world for the first thirty-seven years of my life. But then a reversal occurred, and I turned about and changed direction. In that dramatic shift I became no longer a microcosmic speck of the universe plodding the occidental highway, instead I had become a macrocosmic vehicle, helping to carry the universe along on its neverending course.

I had turned about, my journey had shifted from west to east, from coagulation to expansion, and only then did I realize that to cease walking in a singular direction, is to become all directions.

This metamorphosis began during the night of my thirty-seventh birthday. That night I dreamt a dream in which a man was being strung upon a cross and crucified, but just before he was about to die, the nails which had been driven through his wrists into the cross suddenly gave way and he came plummeting back down to earth. At this point in the dream an intense bright light took over, and a woman's voice spoke, saying "Now we are going to study the inner light, the *om*". And I awoke.

The message of the dream was clear to me instantly: I had completed my journey along the path of the western way, and now my soul had turned about and was heading eastward.

Without a doubt this was a harbinger of all that was to follow over the next couple of years, for in a single moment I had somehow spun metaphysically about, and was now headed the other way. Like a ship which sails out into the uncharted sea for a great duration, but then in an instant turns about and points towards its home port, I was no different than I had been the evening before. Only now I was headed home.[1]

I was now charting a course away from the perils of multiplicity and the mundane, and was bound for the great void of the eternal self wherein lies that peace which can come only after a long, challenging journey comes to completion beneath a beneficent constellation. And from there the soul charts a different course, into different waters, out of the raging northern seas, and into the placid waters of the One. This is when the wayfarer, lost

---

[1] I had already received the portents of such a shift from two earlier dreams: one in which a great spirit had come to me and told me that after the crucifixion Christ had gone to Tibet. I know now that, despite conventional biblical records, the reality is that Christ did not die on the cross, but instead survived the crucifixion, and afterward journeyed to Asia, where he became known as Issa.

In another dream Christ himself appeared to me and pointed to a scene in which an oriental woman was in a wheelchair, and when I awoke I knew that Christ had been pointing at me- my inner, female, eastern self who was disabled. However, soon she was going to be prodded to get up and walk. That is- I was about to uncover her within myself.

for so many years in the foreign realms of being, returns again to the beginningless home, to that great cosmic peace which is the *om*ega from which, and towards which, all similar spirits have roamed.

I had been tangled in the occidental drama for many years preceding this shift, and had gone as far as I could go within that limited theater. And so I had to transform, as we all must transform, since change is the nature of the manifest, and therefore to not transform in this life is to have to leave this life and once again take on the perils of re-entry into another life through another womb, so as to become another form which can then try again to transform. What we call death is simply an inability to transform. What we call life *is* transformation.

In fact soon after my shift eastward began I had another dream in which I was told that the ego kills a person if it thinks he or she cannot, or will not, evolve further in this life. The ego in this case is not our identity, but rather our *daemon*, which is the invisible force within us which compels us towards our highest destiny. The *daemon* is necessary and ruthless, often requiring from us an ongoing inner metamorphosis. For if a snake cannot or will not shed its skin it must die from the claustrophobic strangulation which comes from its own inability to transform.

In this case our worst enemy is our own self, and the only way to defeat the inner enemy is to keep growing, keep changing, keep expanding and shifting into the next stage.

It is impossible to get away from such a mandate, because you *are* the mandate. There is no chance of escape from the law of transformation. Change or leave, that is the law. And so you have to keep dying and being born again in life, if you want to avoid being murdered by your own inner God.

As I said, I had gone as far as I could go along the occidental highway. I came to the end of the road and a great chasm opened up before me. As I stood there, teetering on the precipice, not knowing how to go onward, the ego- my inner *daemon*- began nudging me from behind, and I was left with only two options- to fall into the space and be killed, or to die into and *become* the space.

I was pushed but I did not fall. Though neither did I fly. I dissolved. And in that dissolution I expanded beyond the chasm laid out before me.

Until such an inner expansion as this occurs, an individual is confined within the worldly paradigm of existence. There is no way out, and there is not supposed to be a way out. Life in this world is an alchemical vessel- an enclosed laboratory wherein newly created entities can be tried and tested- and it is only by confining the individual's drama within a limited paradigm that the greater forces can choreograph the necessary situations and events which manifest transformations within the soul. It is for this reason that life in the world feels often so wretchedly painful and claustrophobic- because it is. Without such limitation the soul would not evolve into the perfection of which it is capable; just as a fruit tree must be pruned so as to bear the most fruit possible, so too the individual must be spiritually 'cultivated' by the cosmic gardener, so as to bring to earth the greatest bounty possible. However, after having arrived at one's furthest paradigmatic actuality, the soul can no longer find room to grow within the worldly paradigm. That is when the inner dissolution, expansion, and liberation occur. That is when the walls of this realm which had in the past been confining the individual, now become diaphanous and permeable membranes through which the soul can depart and return, at will. The expanded soul can now deliver its new macrocosmic existence into the field of the microcosm. In the words of the Buddhists, the soul has gone from being a *Hinayana*, a lesser vehicle, to a *Mahayana*, a greater vehicle. The cosmos has accomplished its intent. The imprisoned soul has been liberated. And through this individual expansion the entire interconnected universe has grown.

*

three

The subtle chapters of this expansive transformation which I underwent were displayed outwardly through the drama of my worldly existence; I was guided to move through my inner change by being guided to move through the outer world as a mirror to my subtle metamorphosis. That is, I was guided to go on an overseas 'trip', which is a word used aptly both for the call of our inner life, and for our outer journeys in the world, for they are both 'trips'. Thus the drama of the individual is lived through as if in a dream, where the theater of life on earth is the forum in which the microcosmic self grows to its conscious, macrocosmic stature, and awakens beyond the confines of this paradigm. That is when one is liberated, so to speak.

My trip from the microcosm to the macrocosm, from the occident to the orient, began in the occidental land of my ancestors, in the place from which the heart of my western bloodline had originated- Europe.

On this trip I was accompanied, as per usual, by my *soror*². We began our journey on the westernmost outpost of the ancient western world, arriving on the Dingle Peninsula, west coast Ireland, on a drizzly, cool October afternoon. We had gone there because we had been guided to do so. That is all we knew. And so we came as pilgrims who are called to a remote destination for unknown reasons must always come- we came to stay indefinitely. Which is to say, we came to stay until it was time for us to leave. When that was to be we had no idea.

This type of open-ended attitude is a singular rule of thumb for following the call of the spirit; to follow such a call requires the surrender of all expectations and desires until the unknown mission is completed.

In the past I had gone to many places for reasons which were unknown to me until I arrived there. I often made these journeys because I felt intuitively called, or I had a powerful dream suggesting that I undertake the expedition. However, never before had I been called to such a beautiful, comforting, and pleasant place as Dingle Town.

Having been directed to venture to such a place, I cannot help but solemnly envision the Jesuits and missionaries of old, who were sent or called out to dark, foreboding, insect-infested, primordial places on earth such as the Congo Basin, the Upper Amazon, Vanuatu, the Pribilof Islands, northern Canada, or any similar places where the cost of following one's spiritual vocation was never less than loneliness, discomfort, and endless struggle, and often times the price was a great deal more. I think of those stoic emissaries, boiled alive or beheaded for their vocation, and I thank the God within me who, knowing my fragile and stubborn

---

[2] *Soror* is short for *soror mystica* (mystical sister), the female half of the alchemical partnership within which both she and her *frater* (brother) seek individual wholeness, working in mystical cooperation towards that end.

disposition, had the wisdom, compassion, and foresight to send me off to Dingle.

And what a place Dingle is. A town thick with beautifully painted ancient buildings, surrounded by rolling green hills on one side, and the great expanse of the Atlantic on the other. To walk around this quaint town and its neolithic vicinity, with the scent of peat fires flooding through the air, is to be transported back into a time when the whole of one's world was no greater than as far as the eye could see. However, having said this, as far as the eye can see, in Dingle, is farther than the eye can see from many other places on the globe.

Upon taking a brief, one hour hike up one of the bald hills behind the town, and attaining a bit of altitude, a massive panorama opens up, as the northern portion of the peninsula- the Dingle Diamond, as it is referred to in esoteric yarn- displays its bucolic majesty, ancient beehive huts, and gentle country lanes, while the southern view takes in the fantastic breadth of the ring of Kerry, which runs rollicking out to sea and there guides one's sight to the distant, otherworldly Skelig Rocks, the most impressive sight of yearning imaginable for anyone containing even a fragment of a hermit within them.

I have a strong hermit within me, one which has had its fair share of my life so far, but I also have an unbridled reveler. Therefore Dingle Town and its environs was a perfect arena for the operation of both of these inner aspects of myself, as the entire peninsula was historically a center for meditative monks, but is now, paradoxically, a center of raucous ribaldry. Ebb and flow. Yin and yang.

It was into this contemporary social milieu- and not the archaic act of omphaloskesis- which my *soror* and I found ourselves joyfully immersed during our stay on that wonderful peninsula. After all, only a fool would sit alone in a cold, stone room, so as to face the inner demons which had been unwittingly brought to life through the very act of denying oneself some healthy companionship, Guinness, and song, amongst his brethren. And, having been one such repressed, self-mortifier in the past, I say now, better indeed it is to be a sinner than a fool.

With that bit of puerile wisdom supporting our propensities, my *soror* and I launched ourselves into the town every evening, making our way into one or another of the ancient pubs which dot the illustrious area, so as to imbibe a bit of the dark nectar, and be charmed by a fiddle or two.

It could be argued that pub life in Ireland is life as it is meant to be. All other outward actions and events are but interludes or preliminary measures which must unfortunately be undertaken so as to sustain a life which then has the privilege to enter the pub and be fulfilled. For it is here, in the Irish pub, that the spirit and soul, the heart and the mind, the guts and the gonads, the viscera and the vulvas, are all welcome and exercised. It is here that merriment is exalted as the divine characteristic which it truly is. It is here that camaraderie and community, as well as introspection and isolation are noncontradictory events in the holistic panorama of humanity. It is here, on the westernmost outpost of the occidental drama, that humanity has finally arrived at the zenith of its groaning, microcosmic loneliness, and then turned that loneliness into brotherhood and song.

In the past I had revived my spirit many times in Irish pubs, and had been regularly uplifted and transported into ecstasy and enchantment by the goings on therein. However, before spending my voice on overzealous paeans, I regretfully exclaim that, as one who is incorrigibly dissatisfied with the imperfections of humanity's efforts, I have found there to be a large thorn growing chronically out of the Celtic rose that is Irish pub life; it is a thorn which has poked and prodded me and let my psychic blood out onto the stone floor of not a few said establishments; it is a thorn which invites disquiet into the seemingly harmonious goings-on within the fervor of the pub, for in the midst of such music and merry-making …there is no dancing. That is the thorn. For where there is no dancing, there is no heart. And where there is no heart there is only mind. And where there is only mind the cold grimace of stasis and objectivity spill out through the wailing fissures of death and cremate the soul.

Anyone who has sat in on traditional Irish music sessions might encounter the same pain of being elevated ecstatically by such uplifting, soul-grabbing music, amidst a throng of others who are feeling the same inspiring pulse, and yet not a single person is dancing. There is no dancing in Irish pubs. It is unbelievable. A cultural catastrophe. How an entire country, so blessed with the gift and heart for music, can separate their bodies from the exalted rhythm, is beyond me. It is infuriating. To listen to inspired music is one thing, but to dance to it is another enterprise altogether.

Listening is of the spirit, but dancing is of the soul. To listen to music is to become elevated by the music, but to dance to music is to *become* the music.

No matter. There are those of us who, having been lifted into the empyrean vibration of the Celtic riff, eventually cannot, or will not, remain still.

I had sat through countless, indescribably penetrating music sessions in the past, and I had convivially repressed the thump and shimmer I felt in my legs and feet, so as to prevent them from taking off with my body and plunging me forth into an unproprietous pagan dance. However, there came a time when I found myself powerless to withhold the rushing force of glory from overtaking me.

It came on a night perhaps two weeks after my *soror* and I had arrived on the Dingle. As per usual, in the evening we had made our way into one of the town's establishments, had put back a few pints of the dark and delicious tincture, and then had eased comfortably into the ensuing auditory rapture, as a music session began.

But this night was not like other nights. This was a night when the stultifying chains which the entire Irish culture had bound itself within, and by which I had allowed myself to be held as well, suddenly lost all power of constriction and ability to contain, and I found myself lost to the freedom of the soul that knows no law nor reason nor propriety which might prevent that soul from its truest and most desperate expression.

Bullocks to the letter that killeth. I say: when in Rome forget the Romans and do as thou pleaseth.

What happened on that particular night is that the session started like any other session- the music began, people took thoughtful note of it, and the joy of the Celtic muse flooded joyfully, though without visceral effect, through the atmosphere of the pub. But then the truth revealed itself in a startling display. And that truth came in the form of a woman fiddler who did not play the notes in a solely traditional manner, like a verbatim parrot repeating the same old tune over and over again. No, she played music the only way true music can be played. Which is to say, she played from her heart. And my God what a heart she played upon. Let me tell you, the fiddle transformed from the manifest realm of wood and metal, and softened into the ethereal realm where it became the living voice of her resounding inner ventricles, as she soared her way beyond the mainstream, beyond the usual, beyond the practicable, and took that instrument of heaven into the very reaches of her soul and made it sing with a voice that could shatter the moon.

And man was she quick. She was lightning and flesh fused together in an escalating invocation to the grandeur of our divine heritage. She was the spirit of song cascading in a downpour of dexterous mania. She was the held energy of the cosmos suddenly released in a whirling torrent upon the unexpecting pilgrims of the keep. And I... I was done for.

I like to believe that I can dance as fast or faster than any fiddler can play. And I state this delusion not so much out of braggary, but as a challenge; for I will gladly and with great privilege be defeated on the mortal battlefield of the song, if ever I come upon a fiddler who can beat me. And to be sure, at that moment I will be one man who has found victory and defeat in the very same event.

But what happened that night was not a contest, not about speed anyway. If it was, then it was a contest between that heartful woman's violin, and my own equanimity. And yet it was not a contest, it was a massacre. I was destroyed. I was obliterated. There was no battle, no war, no surrender. I lost, instantly. And what I lost was... myself.

As I said, this particular session began like any other session, but it was only too soon apparent- to myself if no one else- that this was no ordinary session. This was revelation. This was the end of what had been and the birth of a wholly new way of being. This was the unchecked, unmitigated, unrehearsed inflammation of the tendons and the heart.

After a few brief moments of trying to hold my own- of trying to sit still and quell the tumult rising within me, and thus affecting a common, controlled enjoyment of the pleasantries of pub life- I came undone. I left my seat, rushed through the throng of idlers, and landed a few feet in front of her majesty. And I danced. My God did I dance. Amongst a crowd who almost instantly became a thundering mob of appreciative spectators, and who instantly accepted my barbarism, and then lifted me further with their hoots, and claps, and screams, and howls, and my fiddler running me up relentlessly into the unleashed reaches, further and further, faster and faster, with no brakes nor bars to hold me, only a flaming fury of unleashed exaltation ensconcing me, as her spirit and song washing into and through me and the notes rising unrelenting, climbing higher and higher and driving me inexorably into an apocalyptic insanity of bliss and insobriety that was born to smash the world in two.

Dancing with abandon, dancing the last dance, the dance that would end in a new beginning, I lost myself into the music until I became a living, manifest expression of the music.

Entering the ecstasy and passion, and breaking through the hold of personhood, I became Nataraja, the Lord of the Dance, an incarnation of Shiva, the destroyer, and I was gripped and wild in the accumulation of all past energies leading to this one emancipative, apocalyptic moment, when the entire history of my lineage and peoples would converge upon the microscopic moment of cosmic transformation where I would rapturously dance out the old rhythm, and rapturously welcome the new.

Dancing Shiva's *tandava*, his dance of destruction, I was destroying myself in an act of agony and celebration. And yet I was creating out of that very destruction. I was dying and being reborn in the same now-moment where Genesis and the Apocalypse meet as one carnal supernova eradicating all that was and creating all that has yet to be.

I danced like a man who had never before danced nor had known of dancing. Or perhaps I danced like a man who had always been dancing all his life, and had never done anything but dance, and yet this was the first time he had become the Lord of the Dance, and so became the dance itself.

I danced the dance my people had been trying to dance for millennia. A dance of agony and ecstasy, a dance of abandon and release. And I danced it.

Without knowing it I danced the dance which destroyed the past so as to reclaim the eternal beginning of now, so as to be that which has not yet been, so as to release my ancestors and become myself, so as to let go of all history, all thought, all memory, all ties, all links, all familiarity and foundation, and to rise out of the tired old design like a novel pattern obliterating the sky.

I danced without fear, without knowing, without anything that had ever existed in me prior to that dance; no longer the me who was there before the dance that destroyed me, I became something that never had been. I broke through, and became new.

I was dancing the karmic dance of newness, stomping and flailing and swinging about wildly in a triumphant expression of an existence which knows nothing of itself but that it is a glory to be alive. A great glory.

When the tune finally ended I was almost dead. Fortunately I had been resurrected, and so I had just enough life left in me to turn spontaneously towards her majesty on the fiddle, and, bowing with hands together in the traditional *namaste*, I gave due honor to the one who had resurrected me from the grave.

Stumbling back to my seat like Lazarus after the resurrection, I sat through the rest of the session in a convalescent stupor of merriment and exhaustion, and sucked back a few more pints of the holy analgesic.

When the music was finally over and the crowd headed out of the establishment, I went up to the one who had danced me out of myself so as to thank her and give due homage. After our cordial salutations, she introduced herself as Efa, making comment that her name was the Gaelic version of Eve. Of course. I should have known. I had been lifted off the ground by the Mother herself. I had entered into Her rhythm, and had been quickened by the Goddess incarnate. No one else on earth could have done that to me but the Goddess Herself, living through the radiance and roar of one of Her own inspired emanations.

I had danced the dance of my spirit on earth, and I had done so to the vibration and rhythm of the earth Herself.

After years of wandering and wondering why it was that I had come to this maddening world, and what it was that I was supposed to do, I had finally landed in the lap of the living Mother, and had been elevated out of an old story and into the revelation of a new song.

Perhaps this world and life would never reveal the true nature of my existence. Perhaps I would continue to be plagued by uncertainties, discontentment, and disquiet. Perhaps I had come to this confounding earth for many reasons which would remain beyond my knowing. But at least I now knew one of them. I had come to dance. *Om, baby!*

*

four

After the exultation came the ennui. I had achieved an inner metamorphosis through an outer experience and now the outer which had spawned the renovation began to pale into a dull shade of torpor. Which is to say that my beloved Ireland no longer exuded a welcoming, inebriating pulse onto my being. I was no longer smitten with the pubs and cheer and foamy tincture which had so captivated me in the past. No, I had danced that dance and now there was no returning.

Luckily for me, as for all of us, the spirit knows more than the mind can imagine. As such I began to have a series of dreams which were pointing me in another direction, and though I did not understand at first, soon enough my perspicacious subconscious caught on to my inability to grasp its messages, and so that omniscient well of symbolic mystery eventually condescended into the linear realm where all things make sense to blokes like me. That is, in the final dream pushing me onward, a voice stated, with blunt, matter-of-fact, for-those-who-have-ears desperation- "You belong in Amsterdam!"

Ah, but of course, why didn't you say so in the first place?

And so, soon afterward, my *soror* and I began a two-day journey from the land of leprechauns to the netherworld itself, the Netherlands. And oh, what a netherworldy, dreamlike, and twilight-realm Holland *is*.

If you have not yet been to Amsterdam then you have not yet lived amongst progressive humanity. You have instead lived only in a prison amongst despots and barbarians; a prison of obsolete laws, compassionless chains, and archaic ideologies. You might as well still be swimming in the murky depths of a pre-cambrian swamp, waiting for your unknown legs to evolve and carry you out of the mire. For at this time, on this earth, the only country which has raised its head up out of the murky depths is Holland. The only country which is guided by intelligence and care, by the mind *and* the heart, is Holland. The only country which guides its citizens instead of persecuting them, and tolerates human needs, instead of condemning these, is Holland. The rest of the world lives under the oppression of fearful, dimwitted men and women who have neither the creativity nor the foresight to lead their fellow men.

Before I had gone to Amsterdam I despised everything mankind had created en masse. I hated every city I had ever encountered. I distrusted every lawmaker and politician. I saw nothing but stupidity, noise, greed, abuse, and depravity. But by the time I left Amsterdam I had fallen in love with cosmopolitan life. I had become the exuberant participant of a city where tolerance, peace, justice, and enlightenment were its motivating factors. I had walked the most charming cobble-stoned streets, canal sides, and alleyways fronted on each side by idyllic, otherworldly- tall as the people in them- organic buildings. I had ambled along major thoroughfares in the middle of rush hour, enjoying the unbelievable silence found in this city whose citizens ride bicycles and trams instead of clogging their world with automobiles. I had basked in the great consciousness of the gentle and aloof Dutch folk. And I had enjoyed the unbridled freedom of cannabis cafés, hash coffeehouses, and magic mushroom 'smart' shops, as they are so appropriately called.

When I left Amsterdam I left with a sense of gratitude that I had never felt for a metropolis before. And to this day I can feel within myself that cosmic cosmolopolis, so peaceful and inviting to the true nature of humanity, a place that holds its privileged visitors in the loving way that humanity deserves to be embraced.

I will say it again because it must be said- Holland is the only country on earth where wholeness and freedom are promoted. Everywhere else is a claustrophobic, anachronistic, inhumane prison.

Anyway, enough of my political trip. A few days into our stay in Amsterdam I wandered into a centrally located coffee shop called *The Baba* to acquire for myself some of the country's finest. After procuring a blessedly rolled reefer of black hash and European tobacco, I settled in upon one of the padded benches amongst the traveling crowd, lit up my cone of Shiva, and began to ease into the vibe. And what a vibe it is.

Having laid to rest the ancient rhythm which I had been carrying in my very DNA up until Dingle, I suddenly found myself open to, and immersed in, the techno, chillout, and lounge music which was thumping through *The Baba*. In fact I tuned into it and became one with this modern form of music almost instantly, which is an odd thing, because I had never paid much attention to electronica and its variations. I had thought this form of music was simply an ephemeral fad running through the younger generation who wasted itself on ecstasy and other chemical stimulants while gathering like a herd of lost sheep in all-night raves. But I suddenly realized that this was not the case at all. I suddenly understood that techno chill, dance, and trance music were generating the very rhythm of the new vibration-oneness. It became apparent to me that all other contemporary forms of music were caught in the web of duality, and therefore were expressions of duality; the duality of lover and loved, of good guy and bad guy, of loss and gain; all rock and roll, country, folk, blues, jazz, rap, and, yes, even Celtic music, were bound into and expressing duality. But not techno. Oh no. Techno brings with it a whole new paradigm- the paradigm of absolute union.[3]

I realized then that I had to finish with the old vibration before I could merge with the new. I had to dance duality out of myself like a mad drunkard screaming a final goodbye to his long dead lover. I had to divest myself with violence and anguish from the vibration I had been born into, had grown up with, and of which I had known no alternative until sitting there in *The Baba*, soaked in the breath of Shiva, with this new rhythm, this new feeling pulsing through every cell and molecule of my soul and body.[4]

I knew then that a massive consciousness shift was underway, not only for myself, but for all of modern culture, and one of its prominent expressions was the fluid, penetrating, non-dual vibration of electronica.

As the universe evolves we must all evolve with it. Often this means that the older generation must learn from a younger one. It is in the spirit and openness of youth that new realities emerge most prominently. And therefore it is only by getting rid of all pride of learning and wisdom- neither of which necessarily come with age- that we can look to the younger generations for a clearer vision of the contemporary spirit.

---

[3] After my joyous relationship began with electronica I then remembered that a few months earlier I had been having dreams in which an acquaintance of mine who was a techno DJ had been making appearances. At the time of the dreams I had no idea what he was representing, but now I see that the subconscious was pointing a finger into the distance and trying to tell me something of what lay ahead, for, without my being aware of it, my inner vibration must already have begun changing.

[4] 'Baba' refers to Baba Ganesha, the elephant-headed Hindu deity who is the son of Shiva and Parvati, and, it is said, is the great initiator of new events and experiences. "How wondrous is the way of God, who appears as an elephant (Ganesha) and activates everything..." *Song of Ribhu* 1:11

It is only in the recognition that everything is always new that we can depart intelligently from all that has been. All foundations which are built must be fluid and in constant change or else they will have to crumble; only that which is hard can crumble; what is soft can ooze into new forms and new dimensions. It is this supple quality of our eternal nature which allows us to live through incarnations in one lifetime. And it is the supple quality which allows us to take upon the new vibration. To hold onto an image of ourselves or the world as if these are absolute realities is to carve a graven image of life into the tempestuous ether, which is to face our own destruction.

To become a fluid aspect of the fluid cosmos is to enter the diaphanous, formless realm which exists eternally in the subtle layer running parallel to the manifest. This is to become the dynamic stillness behind the evolving form.

It is only through practiced forgetting which begets unrelenting novelty that the image of oneself shatters harmoniously into the ether, and one awakens as the undying awareness whose name is nobody and whose image is nothing.

In that twilight eternity where the shift and pull of humanity twinkles softly around and through the all-permeating Self, we expand into dimensions not exhausted by our pretenses. We become that which is beyond becoming. We arrive at where we always have been. We blossom like flowers formed eternally in the cosmic structure of wonder. We shine like invisible rays cast down upon the dark and tremulous apparitions. We glow like molten energy cascading into the receptive ocean that is also the generative source. We actualize a deathless subtlety which denies the duality of time. We fall away from all that is so as to fall into the archetypical domain. We enter a now that is always beginning and never will end. It is a now that is one. A now that is forever. A now that destroys all that is not now. It is a holocaust of reality which sends the blazing formless wind into form, transfiguring all that is into a viscous cauldron of undivided *isness*. We have crossed the line, and in doing so we have dissolved the line. Eternity has poured into the vessel of time. And all is new. *Om, baby!*

*

five

After numerous days of immersing myself in the peace of Amsterdam and the rhythm at *The Baba*, my *soror* and I decided to partake of a wholly different vibration of newness altogether- psychedelic mushrooms.

Ah, Holland! Unlike in other countries, where insulting, inhuman regulations force one to skulk around like a hunted man in order to purchase and ingest the glorious spore, when in Holland one need only walk into one of the Smart Shops, peacefully peruse their offerings, and then exchange a few euros for some legal soma.

After inspecting the commodities, we decided on the smallest and strongest of all, the magic mushroom of Hawaii, and repaired back to our hotel where we ingested and awaited the apocalypse.

But the apocalypse never came. No inner assault, no psychic hazards, no visitation nor communication from the spirit realm. We were each simply whisked away gently on a carpet of love, and led into the knowledge of our truest, Creator selves.

I say this without being able to explain the experience any further, because to get to the Creator within is to go beyond knowledge and explanation. It is to enter the preconditioned realm where newness is ever happening, and nothing but newness, and all that is has never happened before, and because it has never happened before it is ever created, and nothing but new creation ever is, nothing is old, nothing has been, nothing but the newness of what has never been *is*. To get to the Creator self is to destroy history, and to destroy time. The Creator knows nothing of the past, for there is no past. History is a myth of the created, and time is a lie. But to go beyond history and time means to destroy your created self, because your created self is composed of history and time. And so to destroy the lie of time and history is to become the Creator of a never ending newness which is the world but does not belong to the world, for newness belongs nowhere. To get to the Creator self means to die eternally so that you can give birth eternally. This is the beginning which never ends, for there is no end, there is only an eternal beginning, and because of this everything has just begun, and therefore there is no cause nor effect nor karma[5] nor rules. There is only that which has never happened before.

Newness evaporates all things. Newness destroys. Newness creates. Newness is. And that is all, and nothing more can be said of it.[6]

In the creator self there is no 'one' truth, no one way to live, no one rule, there is only the ever-new living now, and our ever-new recognition, response, and re-creation in it.

Newness is the ever-occurring orgasm of life. This universe began with an orgasm, continues due to orgasm, and perhaps will end in an orgasm. After all, though the word climax denotes an end, it is this end that is also a beginning; climax leads to birth. So perhaps the beginning of this world, this plane, this realm, this life, began with the climactic orgasm of creation which heralded also its end. Perhaps all of this has been simply the inexorable fallout of the beginning which began the end.

If this is the case, no doubt the unavoidability of the end which is the beginning is the impetus which causes us to seek the beginningless, so as to not be bound into the conditioned creation which will inevitably end only because it began. Yin and yang, so to speak.

To arrive at newness is to go beyond beginning and end, for that which begins is already over, whereas newness is an eternal now.

To become that which has neither beginning nor end is to become an immortal, self-substantial, conscious eternity.[7]

---

[5] The fire of the spirit will burn your karma away like dead wood becoming ashes; what once was a heap of deadfall in your way, now becomes rich compost for the new seeds.

Karma is an aspect of the past. When the part dissolves and you become the whole, your karma dissolves along with it.

Karma has ended when you are no longer bound to this realm.

[6] "This has never happened before". To say this, and to know this, is to exist within the creatrix, and to be the spontaneous, ever-creating, uncreated manifester who is never apart from the absolute Beginning.

[7] To become beginningless is, in Hindu terms, to become Brahma and Saraswati- the creators who came before the beginning.

To arrive at this beginningless Godhead is a rare event indeed. Even in India, where every aspect of the divine is shown immense devotion and attention, there are almost no temples devoted to Brahma or Saraswati. And this out of hundreds of thousands of temples! The reason must be that very few people are capable of identifying with the creators who came before creation- the beginningless Godhead; it is perhaps because it is so incredibly difficult to move beyond the known that such communion with the primordial parents is rare.

Whereas Vishnu and Laksmi sustain and guide all that is, and Shiva and Kali destroy, Brahma and Saraswati do nothing but create[7]. And so to attain union with this

Embalmed in the immaculate newness of all that is, my *soror* and I left our apartment and took a walk along the canals to one of our favorite vantage points. Along the way, amidst the newness of what had never happened before, we fell into a fit a laughter the likes of which could heal the worst woe of anyone suffering from a past that has never happened.

I mean we laughed the eternal laugh. We laughed and wept from laughing. We walked and laughed. We stumbled and laughed. We stopped from an inability to stumble, and we laughed, and laughed, and laughed.

I have heard it said before that laughter is the best medicine, and I can finally confirm this illustrious observation. There is no sickness or sin that can survive an Armageddon of this type of laughter. There is no chance. There is no sorrow or pain that can withstand this level of cosmic laughter. It is impossible. They are mutually exclusive. A laughter like we laughed brings an end to everything that is not laughter. Everything else is destroyed in the bonfire of irrepressible mirth. I understand how the myth of history and the lie of time are laid bare and then vanish altogether through an onslaught of inextinguishable bliss. And I know how the myth of history and the lie of time begin re-assembling themselves as soon as we stop laughing, and then fall into the false drama where worry and sorrow begin to take root and then choke out the light of laughter altogether.

And so all of life becomes a battle of perspectives, nothing more: to be lugubrious, or to laugh. There is no war in heaven nor on earth that is not fought on this battleground alone, though few of us, if any, know this. Imagine, if you will, armies of men attempting to attack each other while falling down in uproarious fits of laughter. War would be impossible. I hope you see my point, and do not assume I am merely being facetious. Oh no. When the universe comes again to one of its pivotal climaxes, the battle will not be fought between two external enemies, clashing in bloodshed and rage, instead it will take place on a subtle, cosmic soul level. And those who fight the good fight within themselves

---

remote aspect of the Godhead is to become the creative, unrestrained orgasm arising between the beginningless Mother and Father; we are their newness without a history. That event is now.

will be the only true victors. They will leave the battlefield of the myth of history and the lie of time. And they will be laughing.[8]

*

six

It was not long after our release from all-that-is-not-laughter that my *soror* and I somberly rejoined the realm of time and schedules, and flew back to Vancouver.

Arriving in Canada after our time in Europe was like descending from an otherworldly levity into the thick soup of the lower vibration that *is* North America. On the bus from the airport I had the despairing recognition that the 'new world', as it is so inappropriately called, is still but a cultural colony of Europe, and continues to lag way behind its cultural ancestor; whereas Europe is flying off in fifth gear, speeding forward on a direct course to unity and oneness, North America is chugging along in second, barely making headway against anachronistic realities and political divisions.

It was a troubling awakening for me to arrive back in the place I called home, and feel the sluggish cultural rhythm, and the overbearing psychic clime of the ambient, viscous consciousness residing therein.

I quickly realized the only way to survive the winter in the torpor of Canada without losing all I had gained in Holland was to sequester myself in our little apartment, and become an inner-city monk. I had to hold and become the space which had been effortlessly given to me in Amsterdam. Which is to say, I had to become *om*.

I abandoned almost all societal ties, and spent my days painting, playing music, and meditating in the expansive radiations of the *om*.

In the beginning was the sound, and the sound was *om*. It is the sound of contemplation, the sound of unity, the sound of

---

[8] It is this lack of 'time' which Christ acknowledged when he stated: "Before Abraham was, I am."

home. And the sound became manifest, and dwelt amongst me, and became me.

I realized that the music of life, the *om*, is always playing. The only choice is whether to move and dance to it, or to not dance. But actually there is not choice, there is merely an ultimatum- dance or die.

To dance while not dancing is to invoke the music. To be while not-being is to become the *om*.

In many hidden ways we are always seeking the great radiance of the *om*, which is our true nature, whether we know it or not. To be inside the *om* is to unite with the undivided. To be outside of the *om* is to be separated from the all, which is to be crazy.

The *om* is the inner light which radiates the drama. The *om* is where creation and destruction are the same eternal now pulsating event. *Om* is eternally new, eternally *now*, and is always happening. *Om* is thus beyond any experience, but is *also* every experience.

To sit still and empty for lengthy durations, is to become a motionless transformer of the pulsating now, through which the separate threads of form and energy are re-woven, transmuting the dull lead of mundane existence into the psychedelic throb of the living gold, which is One, the *om*.

To be the *om* is to create God out of the elements, which is to know and to be and to contain all aspects of the now singular God. To know no other, but only the dynamic qualities of the Self which is one. To know that Self. To be that Self. To know and to be.

In the nothing self which is Self, there the living *om* generates its own occurrence as all that exists, and does not exist. All duality ends in the ever-now-beginning orgiastic center where creation and destruction are merely an instantaneous newness called the one-flowing change, beyond the division of life and death.

In that *om* space we are glorified in the eternal unmoving stream.

Beyond faith and fear lives the ever-conscious dream-self, forever smiling behind all that is. She within he. He within she. Creation is this fertile union of wholeness; to know and to be; the I and the you, which are one; the not-something which is, and the somethingness which is not. Spirit and flesh. The bride and the bridegroom. Love.

To know and to be one. No me, and no other. One.

In the living *om* beyond division I am stillness and I am change, and there is no difference. I am the space which upholds the form, and I am the form as well. I am home, and I am *the* home. I am eternity.

I am the all because the all is undivided. I am the all because there is nothing but the all, and that all is *om*.

In the *om* I am the primordial and the present. I am the essence and the shape. I am in and of the *om* which is the transparent exaltation of the glory expressing itself. I am that glory *om* which is beyond time and thought, beyond self and other, beyond name and knowing.

I am sitting in the *om* but there is no sitter nor sitting, only the *om* radiating the original vibration of the self prior to its dance into selves. I am the self dancing into self, the *om* making *om* of the world, the world returning to *om*, the fecund mayhem copulating without abortion through the intrepid eructation of the sound that is light that is being.

It is the *om* that is I, the *om* that is am, the *om* that begins and remains after all that is expressed dissipates away from its origin and is swallowed again and excreted as *om*.

In the void that is no void, the sound that is our silence, the eternity that is our now, the life that is our being, we re-sound through the echo of the *om* which does not begin nor end but is the archetypical substratum of the harmony within.

At the quintessence of all thought and action, behind the struggles and perils of all purpose and hope, beyond the tears and the folly, the sorrow and the joy, the coming and going, the inner and the outer, remains the never ending song that births all fragments into the cosmic muck to sink and grow and lift and strive towards what is never far but always beyond every effort to arrive. For to arrive at the *om* is to stop. To stop is to end. To end is to be still. To be still is to enter the void of creation.

In the silence of that living void exists the resounding *om* which begets the universe. And we are that. *Om, baby!*

A Sri Yantra, by the author
The Sri Yantra is the visual expression of the sound of *om*. This pattern is seen in deep contemplation by monks chanting the *om*. It has also been recorded electronically as a pattern which emerges during the sound of *om*. This picture includes personal additions which are not components of a traditional Sri Yantra.

*

seven

In that eternal stillness I spent the winter embracing the living *om*. It was perhaps because of this that as springtime arrived I felt drawn to return once again to the home of *om*, Mother India.

And so, after putting things in order over the next couple of months, my *soror* and I booked flights headed for the

Motherland, with the intention of staying on the subcontinent from the beginning of August until the middle of October.

All was set in place and the trip was about to begin. However, as my *soror* was also the mother, at that time, of a ten-year old boy, her heart-strings, bound inextricably to her child, were often painfully hard to stretch great distances for any lengthy period of time. In the past she and I had traveled together many times, and had been away from Vancouver, where her son lived with his father, for a couple of months at a time. But it was always a sorrowful and agonizing event for her to depart with me and leave her son in the care of her ex-husband. And, to be sure, the same agony and worry were visited upon her as the day of our departure grew near, an agony and worry which grew to a crescendo of anguish at the thought of not seeing her child for the next two months.

The morning we were to leave, we arrived at the airport and the gravity of the moment became too much for my *soror*. She came undone, admitting, in great sorrow, that she would not be able to join me on our journey; she could not leave her son again for such a lengthy time.

This was a horrible moment for both of us, because we realized that this meant that now we would be separated for those two months, since I could not give up the call of my spirit, and would go on to India without her.

After an agonizing hour of tears and hugging, it was time for me to go through the check-in gates, and, after our last desperate hug, I turned to leave her, but at that moment something switched within my *soror*, and that was …she suddenly knew she had to go.

Whether it was the intense love-bond between us, which caused her change of heart, or the fulfillment of a destiny she could not avoid completing, is a matter not worth debating. She had decided to come, and, having called her son to tell him she would return early if necessary, she and I headed to the gates.

It was at that moment that the cosmos declared its victory, as it always does when a person chooses his or her highest path, and turns down the darkened fork in the road, not knowing where it will lead, but knowing it is the correct path.

At every moment in life there lies a similar fork in the road: one direction leads to one's highest destiny, the other leads to a banquet of consolations. To choose one's highest path at every moment is to sacrifice everything at every moment for one's highest path, but then to also realize that when one is willing to make the sacrifice, the sacrifice is unnecessary, and only that which one is not willing to sacrifice must be sacrificed. This is the lesson of Abraham and Isaac, where at the last moment of the willing sacrifice of his son Isaac, Abraham was acquitted of the debt, because it had been paid through his will. The debt is our attachment to anything which comes before our inner godself, and the payment is exactly that to which we are attached.

Anyway, my *soror* and I must have both cleared our divine debts, so to speak, for as we were about to go through the check-in gates at the airport I heard a woman call out my name, and I turned to see who it was, and there before me stood an emanation of the Mother Goddess. I kid you not. She was not Efa, the Irish Eve, but another form of the Goddess altogether.

This woman was made of flesh and blood and sweat and love and tears, like all the rest of us. And, yes, she was human. But all of humanity is an emanation of one oversoul or another. We may think we are 'individual', but in reality there is no such thing, for we are all aspects of a greater soul, and each greater soul has many emanations on earth.[9] And the woman who beckoned me just as we were headed through the gates, just moments after my *soror* had chosen the harder but better path, had been pointed out

---

[9] This is going to be a dastardly hard observation to relate, but I will do my best. I have borrowed the word oversoul (or, overself) from Lobsang Rampa, who has written many esoteric books. I'm not certain I believe anything of what he says, but he used that word- oversoul- to describe the exact same pattern which I had been witnessing but had not yet placed a term on it. Therefore, from my standpoint, the body which we possess is like one arm of a many armed, invisible octopus. Each arm is an emanation from the octopus, just as each individual soul is an emanation from the one oversoul. There are many oversouls now on earth, but there are many more emanations, for each oversoul has perhaps hundreds of emanations. I believe that the various emanations are used to occupy different geographical areas of the earthly drama, and so emanations from the same oversoul, or overself, rarely meet each other, and even if they do these emanations rarely recognize each other. However, I have been witnessing this event for many years now, and in my previous book, *IN AND OF*, I described this very same event using the terms 'spiritual archetypes' for the oversoul and 'types' for the individual emanations. The 'archetype' is the invisible oversoul, the 'type' is the manifest emanation, the individual. To meet another emanation from the same oversoul as yourself, is to meet yourself in another body, from another place, living a different life, with unique challenges and altogether dissimilar happenings around them. However, they are the same being as you. Often the two emanations do not look all that similar to the gross vision, but if your gaze is softened and you can see through the spiritual eye, the true essence beneath the form will no doubt betray their similarity. I have met a few emanations which belong to my oversoul- the greater soul which occupies many 'separate' bodies- and these are cosmic brothers of mine, because they are me though in a different body.

to me many years earlier, by an incredibly lucid friend of mine, as an emanation of the Mother Goddess. And there she was- inexplicably, synchronistically, fantastically present to send us off with a smile and a hug and herald the beginning of what would become a life-altering trip for both my *soror* and me.

We had received the Mother's blessing. And all you can do when a benediction like that walks into your life, gives you a great glorious embrace, and then releases you away onto your sacred journey, is to throw up your arms in awe and gratitude, and shout out Hallelujah! That's all you can do. And then you board the plane and go forward.

*

Part II
TRANSCENDENT SPIRIT, IMMANENT SOUL

"Uno itinere non potest perveniri ad tam grande secretum."
(The heart of so great a mystery can never be reached by following one road only.)

one

    I look back now and realize that I could never have imagined what I was in for when I set the ball in motion, many years earlier, by tangling in the spiritual realm and therefore walking straight into the mystery of mysteries, and knowing nothing of what that implied.

    To enter the mystery of self, of the world, of life, and of God, is to set a course into the nether reaches of this dream actuality. It is to enter the implausible archetypical layer of myth and miracle. To enter the mystery of the all is to stand upon a molecule hovering over an infinite abyss.

    To widen one's view of this ineffable life is to enter an infinity which is as obscure as it is bewildering. To enter into this impossible collage of improbability and unpredictability is to dive into a universe whose name is chaos. To dive into chaos is to become chaos. To become chaos is to become uncontrollable. To become uncontrollable is to be free. To be free is to enter into the mystery of self, of the world, of life, and of God. And so the wheel of time rolls on and on, and the magical presence which hides behind the invisible screen knows nothing of itself as other than all that is, and so refuses to halt the glory of its limitless emanations.

    Our meeting with an emanation of the Mother Goddess at the airport in Vancouver was shortly followed by another magical encounter of a similar ilk.

    After arriving in Delhi, my *soror* and I soon learned that the monsoon rains were exceptionally relentless at that time, and had wiped out a few railroad tracks in the north, and therefore no trains were running towards our first destination, Dharamsala. At the moment I heard this news I remembered having a dream a few days earlier while still in Canada in which I was told there were no trains going to Dharamsala, to which I had responded "Oh well, we'll take an overnight bus instead."

    Now, let the reader understand that I had taken many, many overnight buses during previous travels within India. And let the reader know that if there is a purgatory on earth, then it is manifested on overnight bus trips in India. And if you are a bony, six-foot fellow like myself, the journeys are absolute torment.

    I believe I had the dream of which I just spoke because I had openly declared prior to this trip that I refused ever again to take another overnight bus ride in India. I had laid down my gauntlet and the universe rose to destroy it.

And so I took a deep breath, shrugged off my discontent, and my *soror* and I bought tickets for the next night's departure. Twenty-four hours later we boarded the rolling box of horror with a handful of other tourists and a gaggle of Indians.

Soon after we were in motion I realized that I had been on many painful and worrisome bus rides in India in the past but, compared to this one, those others were like magic carpet rides through the Elysium fields. Not only were the two of us scrunched into the first two seats of the bus, where my knees began to rub down into raw stumps from the wall of the driver's cab which lay directly in front of us, but, furthermore, the driver himself was an absolute maniac. We were going to die. I could feel it. Never have I been on a bus in which the man behind the wheel has absolutely no sense of the rules of the road; he knows only the gas pedal, and the horn, and everything else is not worth noting. I was terrified. I admit it. But fortunately I was supposed to be terrified. I was supposed to lose my inner equanimity and faith in divine providence, and I was supposed to realize such a level of danger and discomfort that my *soror* and I finally made our way to the back of the bus where we located two empty seats and there took refuge knowing that we now had twenty seats ahead of us to buffer the impending head-on collision.

But then something very odd took place: as soon as we moved to the back of the bus the driver suddenly calmed down; he became another man altogether. The nightmare had ended.

I believe he calmed down because it was no longer necessary to drive like a suicidal madman; he had only been used as an instrument by the spirit with the intent to scare the living shit out of me so that I would take refuge at the back of the bus so that I could then meet the person who was now sitting right in front of me, who was one of my emanations. Yes, he was me, only different, but the same as well. From different parts of the world we were, but we were one. And after getting to know each other we found we had very similar interests, similar dispositions, and similar souls. No doubt this was the case, because we had the same soul, which is an outcome of being emanations from the same oversoul.

In years previous I had met my Native Indian self on the west coast of British Columbia, my gay self in Vancouver, my sprite-like self in a young man whom I worked with for a while, and now I had met my German self on the way to Dharamsala.

This fellow- my emanation brother- was traveling with a buddy from Germany, who, interestingly enough, was an emanation from the same archetype as a friend of mine whom I had been trying to get together with just before leaving for India. Unfortunately obstacles had prevented the engagement. Though now all of the sudden there we were together, in two different bodies, half way around the world, but to be sure the energy connection had been completed.[10]

I spent the next few days hanging out with my German emanation and our common brother, and we shared music and laughter and conversation about esoteric patterns such as the one I have just described, and then my emanated brother and his buddy departed from Dharamsala, and my *soror* and I were left to the emptiness of that sacred town.

I say emptiness, but I do not mean absence. In the west we have learned to equate emptiness with vacuity, loneliness, torpor, or ennui. But the emptiness of the Tibetan Buddhists is a completely different void altogether; it is a substantial, uplifting, expanding, peaceful, fulfilling emptiness.

This was my third trip to Dharamsala, and on each successive visitation I have fallen more and more in love with this sacred landing pad of emptiness. But then, you'd have to have a soul made of lead and a spirit made of phlegm to not love Dharamsala, for, in addition to the emptiness, the main part of town is thick with good vibes, good food, and spectacular scenery.

On past visits to this hallowed village I was not yet capable of experiencing the great emptiness which lies dense as soup within the walls of this Tibetan Buddhist enclave. But this time it was unmistakable.

---

[10] There are a great many hidden patterns in the sublime realm. One which I often recognize is that friendships and intimate relationships are generally created because the bond between the two 'individuals' is actually a bond between the overselves- the spiritual archetypes- and so the individuals cannot help but come together in friendship or love. I have recognized this time and again, where I would meet a pair of friends, or a man and woman in love, and the two of them would be the exact same emanations ('types' of the 'archetypes') which I had previously witnessed in others whom I had met earlier in life. Once again, this is *not* a logical way to understand the world; not, at least, within the linear, materialistic paradigm which wholly mis-explains the true nature of our undivided selves living within this realm. To see beneath the form, into the spirit and formless patterns which create relationships, is to understand the greater, energetic nature of our human bonds.

Every afternoon my *soror* and I made our way to the main temple or monastery. Once there we would take up the lotus position and enter into the pristine emptiness contained within these sacred places due to the sedulous efforts of the Tibetan Buddhist monks, ever meditating, ever awake, ever alive, ever empty, and ever present.

To experience the immense emptiness which the Tibetan Buddhists are slowly integrating into this realm of form is to enter the formless. And to go to Dharamsala and to sit within the precinct where so many dedicated souls have been expanding into that emptiness, while living in this world of form, is to enter a welcoming void which requires no effort to arrive at, no obligation, no shaved head, and no crimson robe- for the emptiness to be found in the temple and monastery of Dharamsala is ever present, and one need only walk into it with an open heart and a clear mind and the work is done.

I make this claim now because this is what I experienced. Though, as I have said, this was my third visit to the sacred town, and on my first two encroachments I experienced no such profundity. But, then, I may not be the quickest learner in the world: it took me four extended trips to India before I finally received what India had to give; it took me the same number of trips to Europe before I was capable of imbibing some of what Europe had to offer; and it took me many sojourns out into the wilderness before I could receive the glory of that domain. I may be slow, but I am determined.

I had therefore grown more capable of entering the emptiness over the years succeeding my last visit to Dharamsala, and had opened myself to the extent that I was capable, and thus I could receive more of what was available to be received. Furthermore, my kundalini had been active all winter while I was living in Vancouver as a hermit, and this later helped precipitate my awakening to the profound emptiness to such an extent that one evening in Dharamsala I awoke in the middle of the night and it seemed as if I had been cognitively decapitated, for I had the feeling of having no head- I had become one with the great cosmic emptiness; my crown chakra had evaporated. In that deep, ubiquitous stillness the upper part of my being had vanished and I had become one with the nothingness. I had become the emptiness, for the I that I had been was gone, and only the singular, undivided, pristine emptiness remained.

I fell back to sleep, my crown chakra re-assembled, and I awoke the next morning feeling more like my individual, limited self once again. However, the emptiness remained in the atmosphere, waiting patiently for my effortless attention.

A few days later my *soror* and I made our way to the main temple, as per usual, and we sat down near a few monks who were reading and chanting from the holy books.

It was then, as I sat motionless, with the empty monks chanting sacred mantras on my right, and my *soror* sitting close by me on my left, that I experienced the union of emptiness and form, or, rather, the presence of both emptiness and form; I became the common ground between these two realms. I was receiving the feeling of the great cosmic void from the monks on one side, and the sense of the great earthly density of flesh from my *soror* on the other. Emptiness and form became the separate yet united halves of my being; the Great Absence, and the Great Presence- one.

I knew then that we are emptiness *and* form; one half of our being is the cosmic emptiness, the other half is the form.

We are the emptiness pervading all form, and the form impregnating all emptiness.

It is for this reason that the sacred mantra of the Tibetan Buddhists is *om mani padme hum*. *Om* is the great emptiness, and *hum* is the actualization into form. *Om mani padme hum* is the method by which the spirit and flesh are united.[11]

Om mani padme hum describes the descent of the cosmic vibration, the *om*, the alpha, into the worldly realm, the *hum*, the omega.

In *om* we live, and breathe, and have our being, and in *hum* we *are* that being.

Om is everything, *hum* is anything. *Om* is the I, *hum* is the AM. I the eternal, AM the ephemeral. I the formless, Am the form. I the spirit, Am the flesh. *Om mani padme hum*.

---

[11] This mantra is often translated in linear fashion into English as 'Hail the jewel in the Lotus'. This is an unfortunate catastrophe, since the mantra has far deeper and infinitely more profound esoteric implications than this translation would betray. The mantra describes the path from the cosmic to the worldly- from the infinite to the finite- in which the great emptiness is condensed into human dimensions, and therefore can be effective in transforming not only the individual but humanity at large. It would be foolhardy of me to attempt here a more detailed explanation of this mantra, as I am wholly unqualified to do so. Instead, I would highly recommend the book *Foundations of Tibetan Mysticism*, by Lama Anagarika Govinda, for anyone interested in an immensely profound and readable interpretation of this sacred mantra.

Inner and outer meet in the stillness of *om*, and in the activity of *hum*. *Om* is the witness, *hum* is the witnessed. *Om* the ether, *hum* the air. *Om* the theater, *hum* the play.

When emptiness unites with form the cosmic *om* attains the earthly *hum*, and God is born into isness.

The union of these two seemingly opposed realms is the experience of Avalon[12], which is cosmic wholeness. In order to bring this mythical event into our own existence- for Avalon is not a physical place, it is a metaphysical union- we must all dive down into the deepest reaches of the flesh, and we must all rise into the furthest expanse of the great space. We are the bridge between the formless and the form, between consciousness and matter, and between emptiness and love. If we don't reach in both directions Avalon will remain a mythical land. If we attain unity with these divided realms, we achieve the union of emptiness and form, of spirit and flesh, which is Avalon. *Om, baby!*

*

two

After our time in Dharamsala was finished and we had received all that we could at that time from the profound privilege of the Tibetan Buddhist holy sanctuary, we left the emptiness and arrived at the fullness of the Golden Temple, Amritsar, home of the Sikh religion, and epicenter of one of the greatest devotional assemblages in the world.

Arriving at the Golden Temple one arrives at an earthly core and zenith of passionate human devotion. For it is here where millions of Sikhs, over the past five centuries, have come, so as to link their souls and spirits into the fulcrum of this religion's quintessential intent. And that intent is devotion.

---

[12] Although Avalon is the name used to describe the mythical island of the Goddess, often associated with King Arthur and the Grail quest, my own experience is that Avalon occurs whenever there is the complete union of spirit and flesh, or, male and female, within the individual. On a macrocosmic level this is felt as the unified vibrations of Christianity (the Father) and Paganism (the Mother), which historically have been almost mutually exclusive, but are now coming together in and through individuals who attain inner wholeness.

The Golden Temple is the supreme manifestation of devotion. Here a person can eat, sleep, bathe, pray, and listen to music any time, on any day, all for free; which is to say, one can *devote* themselves without obstruction.

When my *soror* and I first arrived at the Temple and its gigantic marble compound, I suddenly remembered that a few months earlier I had received a dream of Guru Nanak, the founder of Sikh spirituality. However, I had not recognized who the white-bearded man in my dream had been until I came into the midst of the Golden Temple where countless posters and paintings flaunt his image. Nor had I expected anything of what that dream portended. But, to be sure, the intent of the universe would rise up to meet me, and I would soon realize that I had been called here for a teaching.

We entered the sacred compound of the Temple environs upon our arrival and began circumambulating around the site via the marble walkway which is continually scrubbed and maintained by pilgrims and volunteers who come to this splendiferous site not only to take what they can take, but also to give what they can give.

After a while my *soror* and I sat down beside the holy bathing vat and fell into awe and appreciation for this monumental accomplishment which the Sikhs have created in honor not only of their founding fathers, but also in devotion to the God-guru within each of us. It is this, it seems to me, that is the intent behind Sikhism- the elevation through devotion of each individual into the immortal stature of their divine selves, all of whom are related in that divinity to a brotherhood and sisterhood of all who seek the same.

During that first evening we eased ourselves into the vibration of the holy compound, and then retired to a hotel near the Temple complex. After falling into a slumber I spent the whole night receiving an onslaught of visitations from numerous past Sikh gurus, most frequently by Guru Nanak himself. He had passed from this world four hundred years earlier, and yet his spirit remains around to give guidance and assistance to those who seek it. The only thing is- I didn't seek it, *it* sought me. And ever full of gratitude I am for this.

Upon awaking in the early hours of the new day I knew only one thing- I needed to return to the Golden Temple without delay. And so at four o'clock in the morning my *soror* and I left our hotel and once again joined the legions of Sikh devotees who come any hour of night or day to partake of their spiritually intoxicating Valhalla.

We again circumambulated the compound, immersed within the river of a great, unpretentious crowd, and then made our way amidst the throng into the inner sanctum of the Golden Temple itself.

The first floor of the shiny building was stuffed full with devotees arrayed around the musicians who take turns filling the compound with their live devotional music. We gently made our way through the crowd and ascended the stairs to the second floor where we sat down in the lotus posture amongst the multitudes silently praying or meditating.

I immediately fell into a deep, spacious peace, and in this still state I came into communion with the living, ever-present spirit of Guru Nanak. It was in this subtle state that I then recognized why I had been called back to the Golden Temple in the early hours of the blessed morning- I was about to receive his guidance.

And so I emptied myself as much as I was capable, and a silent discourse between the spirit of Guru Nanak and myself began. During times such as this, information and knowledge are exchanged almost instantaneously, and therefore insight or wisdom can be gleaned without study, effort, or hindrance, for in that ethereal commingling between spirits the interwoven consciousnesses can transfer understandings without the misunderstandings which words so often convey.

It was in and from this holy communion that I realized, through the consciousness of Guru Nanak, what true devotion is, and why it is so important as the modus operandi for the way we express our eternal selves onto this temporal plane without getting caught in the mundane maelstrom.

I came to understand that true devotion is the state in which one acts from and for his or her eternal, higher self, and that only acts generated from this heightened awareness can be delivered onto the earth without causing the individual to 'fall' into the profane paradigm; all acts must be devotional so as to not lose the great free space of the Godself. Without devotion an act is futile, or even worse- a transgression which causes the eternally free Godself to become ensnared in the worldly paradigm. But through devotion we not only save ourselves from such confinement, we also bring God into the world, and so bring the spirit into the flesh.

A devotional act is one which arises while one is conscious of one's Godself, and then the act is orchestrated onto the world as a blessing to quicken all other Godselves. As such, an act of devotion elevates this human realm into the divine, and unites the devotee to the purity of God, which is the purity of their own divine self, and through devotion the lower and higher selves become one and heaven descends upon earth.

The ultimate Golden Temple is the body and soul of any person continuously acting spontaneously and unconditionally from such devotion.

To find out what it is to act with devotion, and to choose devotion in every act, is to bring the great stillness into the shifting manifest.

And so devotion must be brought into the world, not as a tired ritual, but as spontaneous awe and praise for the privilege and miracle of being.

It is in this sense that devotion goes beyond surrender and sacrifice, because devotion is an affirming rather than a negating act, and so devotion manifests God on earth; devotion *expresses* the perfection of the holy inner silence into form and action.

Sacrifice is necessary only when we have forgotten that all is God. With the sacrifice of this erroneous consciousness, we return into contact with God, and with that contact we become one with God, and then we realize that everything is God, and through this we begin to act with naught but devotion, and soon the ego is annihilated into oneness.[13]

It is through such acts, generated by our Godself so as to quicken this human realm into union with the divine, that we become incarnate instruments of our own eternal selves.

It is for this reason that we must walk with devotion, eat with devotion, work with devotion, drink with devotion, play music with devotion, and make love with devotion. We must do nothing which is not an act of devotion. We must become the living stream of devotion cascading down onto this slumbering plane. We must devote ourselves to our highest bidding, devote

---

[13] "Man! Without love there is no salvation.
God dwells in you and blesses you with the gift of devotion." Guru Nanak (*Sri Raga* 1)

ourselves to our truest selves, and devote ourselves only to acts worthy of our divine heritage. Everything else must be cast aside.

Our true relationship to the above lies within; it is only when our relationship to the world overwhelms our relationship to God, that we become Godless and fallen. And therefore, the reason we are Godless is because we desire everything else before God. Godlessness is our choice, not God's.

A similar teaching occurs in a verse from the apocryphal Book of Enoch, in which some of God's children have retreated to a high mountain so as to maintain communion with the divine. It is in this communion that God, the Father, is continually beseeching his children not to return down into the realm of humanity, not to descend to the profane paradigm of false pleasure, false action, false desire, and false intent. For He knows that if they descend into it they will get caught in the matrix of the world's ways, and so never again become conscious enough to awaken to their glorious, immortal selves.

This story is a wonderful metaphor for my experience with the spirit of Guru Nanak. For I have often walked down into the lower planes of consciousness, into the troubling and trapping realm of separation and division. And now I see that once one is there- once one has taken on the flesh, and *become* human- then the only recourse which returns one to the pristine awareness and communion with one's divine, eternal self, is to never 'fall' into the parameters and purposes of this paradigm, but instead to act ever in devotion to, and with, one's unlimited, holy nature. In doing so one remains in this world and yet maintains connection to the divine consciousness, and so expresses realities into the profane plane which are beyond it. This is how we bless this world which we are. Amen.

*

three

Devotion comes in many different ways for each of us, since we are all unique expressions of the one. The hallmark of devotion, however, is whether an act brings us closer to that one, or drives us further away.

There have been many events along my odd and idiosyncratic journey which, on the profane plane, may seem either useless, or even sinful, but were in fact acts of devotion done with fervor and hope that they would lead me closer to freedom, union, and perfection.

One such odd undertaking began years after I had given up smoking tobacco. I had fought against the tug of that poison for quite a long time, and had finally dismissed it for good.

But then, all of the sudden, a number of years later, I had a few dreams in which tobacco was shown to me as a temporary means which would assist me to awaken into a level which I had not yet arrived at. I was admittedly a little uncertain as to the message of the dreams, and therefore did not partake of tobacco right away. However, soon after, and synchronistically enough, I was reading through a book of esoteric information, and the writer made the claim that for those people who have trouble connecting their lower self to their higher self, smoking some tobacco can be of assistance.

With that added bit of information, I plodded off to a nearby tobacco shop, purchased a small cigarillo, and later that evening inhaled a bit of the smoke into my awaiting lungs. Then I sat back and relaxed into myself.

I soon discovered that the tobacco had a relaxing effect and allowed me to sense a greater unity between myself and all things, the outcome of which was a very subtle, and yet profound, peace. This may sound like a bucket of errant hogwash to a world which has determined tobacco to be a carcinogenic calamity, which in fact it is when produced and used in the abusive way it has been by the modern world. However, there is good and bad in all things, and it is only for us to choose which side of the coin we include in our lives.

It is perhaps for the more positive aspect of the sacred plant that North American natives would ceremoniously smoke tobacco in a 'peace' pipe, thereby making it into an instrument for inner peace and for union with the all.

I recall the marvelous story of a wise Native American elder who lived during the twentieth century in the northern part of British Columbia, told to me by a man named Mark who had been a social worker for a year or so on the Native reserve in which this elder resided.

Mark told me that he and the elder had exchanged very little conversation during the year that he was there, for the elder spoke no English, and Mark spoke very little of the elder's native tongue. However, this negligible communication barrier could not prevent more sublime interactions from taking place between them.

This came about during a day when Mark was sitting in sunshine on the outskirts of the reserve, and as he sat there the elder arrived nearby and began throwing his tomahawk at the small stump of a sapling which was used by the villagers for target practice. It wasn't long before Mark recognized that the elder was hitting the bull's-eye every time, from a formidable distance. Apparently the elder had thrown his hatchet perhaps twenty or twenty-five times, hitting the center of the wood perfectly every time. Mark was impressed, and kept his attention on the elder. Soon enough the old wise man turned towards Mark and, though he said nothing, Mark knew the old man was impressing upon him the understanding that he, the elder, was in complete control of the situation, and that the next throw would prove it. The old man then launched his tomahawk and landed it just outside of the bull's-eye, and Mark knew it was an intended throw to show that wherever he aimed his axe, he would hit.

This action of the wise old man was not a prideful display of marksmanship; the elder had something far more important in store for Mark. Immediately after the last throw he then turned towards Mark and sent his spirit and consciousness out, enveloping Mark and uniting the two of them in the ethereal domain. Mark was spellbound, for he knew for certain that they were communicating perfectly and were united as one in consciousness and spirit. Then the elder somehow expanded himself and dissolved at the same time, and Mark saw him completely merge into the environment around him, and Mark knew that the elder and the earth were one. In fact, the elder was one with everything.

It finally made sense to Mark why this old man of the woods could go on hitting bull's-eye after bull's-eye, over and over again: it was because he had become everything- the thrower, the thrown, and the target. He had become the entire world of spirit and matter- the great cosmic Self aware of itself. He had lost himself into the whole, and so had become the whole, and therefore everything he did was in cooperation with the whole. He had crossed the river of separation, and had merged into the ocean of oneness.[14] Amen.

*

four

After the blessed teachings from the subtle spirit of Guru Nanak at the Golden Temple, my *soror* and I moved eastward by train, heading for Rishikesh.

En route we were befriended by a true brotherhood of Sikh boys and men on their yearly pilgrimage to the sacred Sikh sites located in the Garhwal Himalaya. The Sikh fellows formed an amazingly jocular and caring group, ranging from teenage boys to sixty year old men, though no age difference was apparent in their interactions together- everyone was equal, everyone had a voice, everyone was as valid as the next, and everyone was a brother. It was an uplifting collection of souls to witness, containing immense love and wholesome ribaldry.

I soon recognized one man within the group to be the Indian emanation of a very good friend of mine back in Canada. Skin color aside, this fellow could have been my buddy's twin; he walked the same, carried himself the same way, showed humble love and respect for the rest of his brethren the same way, and took to me in the same way as well. He was the exact same spirit, in a different body, as my buddy back home- fifteen-thousand kilometers away. And yet he was right there, with me. It was fantastic. I was amongst my brothers. The fact that I did not know any of their names mattered nothing at all, for siblinghood is an outcome of the soul's affinities, and not of the mind's conceptions.

Our train journey ended at Haridwar, which is about twenty kilometers south of Rishikesh, from where one must continue by rickshaw or bus. Haridwar was a disorienting sea of

---

[14] It is interesting that the literal definition of the word 'sin' is: to miss the mark. In this case, as in all cases, missing the mark is simply mis-understanding the universe as a divided cornucopia of individual events and beings, rather than as a oneness devoid of separation. The old man could hit the mark every time because he did not miss the mark- he did not recognize separation, only oneness.

pilgrims at that time of year, and the area outside of the train station was a maelstrom of chaos and confusion. Luckily we were invited into the circle of the Sikh brotherhood, and, following their lead, we proceeded through the tightly packed throng on the town's main thoroughfare.

On the day of our arrival the entire town of Haridwar was a thick bustle of pilgrims from all over India who had come at this auspicious time to bathe in the Ganges. And what a bath it was.

I had been to the Ganges before, farther down its course along the low lying, central plains, on earlier trips to India, and had decided never to bring my body near that flowing vein of sewage and pestilence. But up the river, closer to its source, at Haridwar and beyond, the Ganges has yet to journey down the mountains and through the endless towns and cities which pour their waste and garbage into it, and so it maintains much of its pristine quality.

Given this incentive, and finding great joy in the frenzy of the entire town bathing and playing about in the sacred water, my *soror* and I could not pass up the invitation of our Sikh brothers to join them in the dunking. And what a baptism it was.

The combined mania of the endless crowd along the ghats, the inexhaustible exuberance of our mates, and the tremendous fury of the Ganges itself, roaring majestically at that time during the monsoon, made for a breathtaking plunge into the torrent which almost tore the shorts off one's buttocks and ripped away the hold upon a brother's hand. Luckily the ghats in such areas are fitted with long chains, secured to the shore, and running out into the river. Holding onto these chains the entire troupe of our brethren would merge together, and we'd make our way out into the surge and thrust of the heaving river, grappling to hold onto each other and the chain, and then dunking under to complete the mission, and then up again, and the resounding laughter of our foster family dancing harmoniously with the blessed violence of the Ganges, and then another dunk, farther out into the flow, and holding desperately and with glee onto a brother's hand, who holds onto another's, and their's is on the chain, and the whole mad show is flipping and whirling about in the pitch and swell, and I can't believe I'm finally in the Ganges, finally soaked in the glory of India's greatest show, finally immersed in the bubbling tempest that is the lifeblood of all that is the real India.

I have crisscrossed this sacred subcontinent numerous times before. I have traveled north to south and east to west. I have slept in the filth and futility of the worst cities on earth, here in India. I have prayed and meditated in the holiest centers in the land. I have walked about as if spell-bound by the people and the impossibility of this maddening and mythical country. I have wept and cursed here. I have praised and given thanks here. And I have lost my mind and gained my soul because of this terrible and holy place. But for the first time in all of my adventures and misadventures within this hallowed, inimitable, inconceivable divine creation, I know that as I am being licked by the fervor of the Ganges, and held by the hand of a brother whose name I do not know, whose language I do not speak, and who I will never see again after this afternoon has ended- I am finally in India.

I am finally in India. I have been baptized into the kaleidoscopic Hindu spirit and vibe by a band of Sikh strangers. I have been whisked out of one great devotional theatre, and transported into another. I have been given Hinduism by the very pariahs who turned against Hinduism, who turned against the caste system, and who grabbed me out of the ethereal dimension of the Sikh society, and launched me into Shiva's soul.

I am finally in India. I have come home. *Om, baby!*

*

five

After parting from the benevolent Sikh brotherhood later that day, my *soror* and I struggled against the raging crowd of pilgrims in Haridwar, and hailed a rickshaw to take us the rest of the way up the road to Rishikesh.

Ah, Rishikesh, what a place! What an unbelievable, sanctified, prayer-ridden, blessing-filled, exalted, monumental accomplishment of the human spirit.

Although the main part of the city is as horrible as every other city in India- and horrible is as gentle an adjective as one can find for such places- as always the gem is to be found within or nearby the shit. And with Rishikesh the gleaming emerald of the spirit lay just out of town, by the bathing ghats, an area which is one of the most frequently visited holy places in the entire country. And there is good reason for such a mecca.

This part of Rishikesh means many different things to many different people, but there is a common denominator dwelling within that sacred area which is the wellspring of everyone's individual experience. The great draw and immense gem of this part of Rishikesh, however, is not to be found in the thousands of pilgrims who flock to the town every day to bless and be blessed by the sacred Ganges, nor is it in the countless shaggy-haired sadhus who populate the town and its environs during a lifetime devoted to meditation, wandering, smoking hash, and begging. Nor is it the intensely soul-uplifting evening *puja* of *bhakti* songs, chants, and prayers carried out at the main temple, which attracts hordes of Hindu common-folk to this divine event every night. Nor is the gem the free food which is given out twice daily to all sadhus, saints, and passers-by at one or another of the philanthropic institutions operating almost invisibly within the area. Nor is the pearl of great price the allure of the Beatles' historic visitations to the town in search of their own enlightenment. No, the gem that is the living, breathing, flowing life of Rishikesh is to be found in and as the sacred Ganges itself. Without the Ganges there would be no Rishikesh. For the Ganges is no ordinary river. In fact, it is not a river at all. It is peace.

Where that sacred artery of the living spirit passes by the bathing, holy ghats at Rishikesh, the river is no longer a mere channel of water moving from the mighty Himalayas, down across the central plains towards its delta in Bengal and Bangladesh. At the point where the Ganges passes the holy, bathing ghats at Rishikesh, the river is transfigured into a standing wave of absolute peace. You can feel it. I felt it, like I had never imagined I could *feel* such calm and serenity exuded from a wildly flowing entity. I had never even thought such a phenomenon existed.

We had come to Rishikesh during the monsoon season, and the Ganges was at its height of fury and flow, and yet there was not a single sense of chaos nor commotion coming from it. There was only peace. And I mean deep, soulful, visceral, corporeal peace. This was not a 'peace of mind', as they say. The mind knows nothing of this peace. Because this type of peace cannot be known, it can only be *felt*. And feeling is the province of the heart, soul, and flesh, and the mind can neither approach nor receive this vibration, and so it must shut off its machinator, and humbly dissolve into the peace which passeth all understanding.

No doubt this immense breath of peace emanating from the Ganges has everything to do with the serene quiescent meditations of the yogis living in caves high up in the mountains near the river's source, as well as the limitless offerings and prayers poured into the water by the endless parade of pilgrims who come to Rishikesh to consecrate their lives and be sanctified by this profound flowing vessel of the spirit.

The Ganges is an actualization of the Goddess Ganga, whom, it is said, refused to come to earth, and so Shiva himself had to come to her and request that she descend to earth to bless this world with her divinity. Apparently she agreed, but the force from her descent onto earth was so immense and powerful that Shiva had to receive her divine plunge from the firmament into the knotted mass of his hair, and there let it flow more gently onto the Himalayas and downward into humanity, where it became the river that is the blessing of Ganga Herself.

In this way Shiva is intricately connected to this divine river of tranquility. It is perhaps for this reason that not only peace radiates from this river, but passion as well, the passion of Shiva; for Shiva is the destroyer who is also a creator. Yes, a creator. And this is because destruction is in fact an act of creation; destruction is the end which is a beginning. As Shiva destroys, his Shakti creates. Shakti is the feminine power of the Godhead, without which only non-being would occur; for divine non-being to transform into divine being, the feminine power of the godhead is essential, for She *is* being. And so it is said that Shiva is nothing without Shakti, and Shakti is nothing without Shiva.[15]

In the union of Shiva and Shakti, the entire universe becomes a dynamic generative commingling of destruction and creation, of heaven and earth, of male and female, of non-being and being, of spirit and flesh. No doubt this is why the most common image to be found in temples devoted to Shiva is the lingam- the symbol of the great penis of Shiva penetrating the yoni of his Shakti.

It is perhaps because of this that one evening after basking in the incredible quiescence pouring off the river, my *soror* and I returned to our hotel and were quickly spirited into our own

---

[15] This line is paraphrased from a wonderful book- *Shiva and Shakti*, by Ganga Somany. Published by Bookwise, New Delhi. 2002

dynamic, generative commingling of spirit and flesh. And by that I mean we made love, Khajuraho[16] style.

It is an incredible thing to merge the duality of male and female into the union of oneness. This is copulation. This is fornication. This is the universe in its creative state of orgasm.

It is an incredible thing to reproduce the fundamental structure of this creative universe through the living actualization of the flesh, which is to orgasm with, into, or because of your mate. And it is an incredible thing to receive her orgasm.

To orgasm is to glory in the fullest rapture of the flesh. To orgasm is to release energy through the chakras, and so to awaken the subtle energies of the kundalini pathway through the gross energies of the love-orgasm. This is to bring the archetypical pattern of the cosmos down into the incarnate potency of humanity. This is spiritual sensuality.

Indeed, the ancient Indians knew that there is little more enjoyable in the cosmic realm of Eros, and little more healing in the earthly realm of flesh, than chomping upon your lover's buttocks, and then slopping about in her loins.

To hold your mate hostage by the clitoris and love is to French-neck with Her deepest soul. To perform cunnilingus as if you were imbibing Amrita- the nectar of immortality- straight from the dewy petal of a vanilla rose, and to go still deeper psychically into the soul of that flesh, to suck on it, devour it, love it and become one with it, is to send the glory of the spirit into the glory of the flesh.

To penetrate your mate in the front-facing wheelbarrow position, and to blow her crown chakra wide open through this tantric practice, is to link Eros with the empyrean beyond, to raise the flesh into the firmament, and so to add fat and fluid, bone and blood, semen and sex into the ledgers of the heavenly roster of divine creations.

To slurp ambrosia from your lover's living, conscious, swollen clitoris is to re-enact the cosmic foreplay, just preceding the Father's orgasm which created all that is.

For though humanity is all too ready to grant women, including the Goddess, the ultimate powers of creation, in fact it is the male aspect of the cosmos which initiates all that is. For a woman can orgasm in the act of union without creating a child, but

---

[16] Khajuraho is the site of some of the most profound and explicit, ancient erotic carvings in all of India.

a man cannot. A man spends his seed and a child is born. A woman orgasms and the universe rejoices. And perhaps this is why a woman, unlike a man, can orgasm in different areas of her loins, in different ways, limitlessly- because the universe wants ecstasy, not *labor*, as this term for childbirth so well implies.

It is indeed interesting that every child born out of erotic pleasure is caused by a man's orgasm, but none from a woman's. A woman's orgasm is the perfection of cosmic rapture; it is the joy of creation, but not creation itself. A woman can orgasm over and over again, out of sheer flesh-joy and pleasure. A man must control his urges or increase his brood.

It is for this reason that a woman in orgasm is the quintessence of the ecstatic, intimate, orgasmic universe itself. A woman in orgasm is the very fabric of this jubilant existence; she is the earth, the flesh, and all matter writhing in the joy of release, abandon, and *being*.

A woman's orgasm is nothing but joy, *because* it is uncreative; it is *om* without *hum*, which is the rapturous vibration of the cosmos unencumbered by its own creation.

A woman cumming wildly from the unrelenting penetration or mastication of her lover is the universe arriving at fruition. Her orgasm is the universe crying out to itself- "Create no more. Enough already. Let us be done with creation, and let us rejoice!" A woman in the emancipated throes of a tremendous orgasm brings light and vindication to the entire mad enterprise of being. Her orgasm is life's validity, its denouement, its manifest perfection. *Om, baby!*

*

six

As well as enjoying the inebriating qualities of the spirit penetrating the flesh in Rishikesh, I was also given a profound awareness of the flesh rising into the spirit.

This came about over the course of many days, and in fact had begun perhaps six months earlier, when, sitting alone in a deep inner peace within my inner-city hermitage in Vancouver, I unexpectedly encountered Krishna's vast space behind my manifested being. This was a tremendously unexpected yet lucid awakening. I say unexpected because I had never paid much attention to the Hindu pantheon, and had only read the *Bhagavad Gita* and a few smaller Hindu scriptures, and I had no thought whatsoever that I was connected to Krishna. And yet there He was, indisputably, in the great deep space behind my manifested being. Which is to say- my greater 'I' awoke as Krishna.

This event made me realize that Krishna was the immense, unmanifest, macrocosmic consciousness behind my being, and Christ was the operational, microcosmic expression of that consciousness.

That inaugural experience six months earlier wore off and drifted into a distant memory for the next while, as I returned to my more limited worldly consciousness which occupied my day-to-day awareness. Then all of the sudden the same awakening returned again in Rishikesh, and I immediately realized this time that Christ and Krishna were the very same being, and that Krishna was my greater, unconditioned self, and my defined and corporeal being was the Christ of that Krishna.

In this way Krishna is my infinite being, and Christ is the finite manifestation of that infinity. And so Krishna is the Great Self of the Christ self, which are one within me.

I realized that both Krishna and Christ are aspects of a singular continuity and, therefore, by becoming both I become transpersonal *and* personal, which is to be the ocean *and* the drop.

This revelation may come as some hard or unbelievable news to orthodox religion mongers, but then they will also find it impossible to swallow the fact that the names Krishna and Christ are significantly similar, denoting a cosmic connection between these beings. And furthermore, the Christianity/Hindu commingling does not stop here, for one of Shiva's lesser known names is Isa, which is uniquely close to Issa, the name for Christ in the East.

I now understand why I had so many dreams in the past in which Christ was shown with dreadlocks, which is exactly the image given to Shiva in India.

I suppose this also accounts for the many times in the past when I would sit still and smoke cannabis, which is what Shiva had done for a mere five-thousand years.

I know now that Krishna is Christ is Issa is Isa is Shiva. Different names for the same cosmic spirit, received in different ways by different cultures during different epochs, but the same eternal great soul nonetheless.

I make this claim categorically, because Krishna states unequivocally in the *Uddhava Gita* that those devoted to him he "...carries across to liberation." The only thing is this- prior to receiving this liberating consciousness, in which I recognized that Krishna was the great macrocosmic space behind my eyes, I was in no way devoted to Krishna; I was devoted only to Christ. But now I know that since Krishna and Christ are the same spirit- one macrocosmic, the other microcosmic, but both aspects of the same being working on the same project of human liberation- to be devoted to one is to be devoted to both, for there is no division, only a logarithmic multiplication of spiritual expansion, in which Christ is the Krishna of this dimension, and Krishna is the infinity of that being radiating out into every dimension, which is the Cosmic Christ.[17]

As my awareness and receptivity increased I became united still further into the incredible space which is Krishna-consciousness, deep inside the cosmic recesses, which then came pouring forth into the Christ flesh of my body.

I became the great, eternal, cosmic ocean of Self which is boundless space, *and* the unique, immanent incarnation which is form.

The whole panoply and chaos now merged into a singular vastness where peace and effortlessness hold sway- a great, reactionless, all-encompassing, ethereal ocean- and I was that ocean called Krishna, and I was the wave called Christ, and they were one.

The ocean of the great consciousness could then pour forth, from the infinite into the finite, from the macrocosm into the microcosm. The KrishnaChrist was complete. The self and the Self, the formed and the formless, the cosmic and the corporeal were one. *Om, baby!*

*

---

[17] I realized only after this experience why the actor Harrison Ford had been showing up unexpectedly in my dreams, as many characters often did. I remembered that most often celebrities or people I knew arrived in the theater of my dreams simply because their name became symbolic of something that name was representing, and the actual person had nothing whatsoever to do with the dream. In this case it became clear to me that Harrison was *Hari*-son (Hari is a name for Vishnu, of whom Krishna was an incarnation. The 'son' is the Christ). Ah but the subconscious is a wise and wily teacher.

seven

The night before leaving Rishikesh my *soror* and I were enjoying the wonderful devotional music and ambience of the evening *puja* at the main temple, and I was so overwhelmed with all I had been given from my stay at this truly holy spot on earth, that I sent out a spontaneous and yet immensely heartfelt blessing to the entire world, immediately after which I heard an ethereal voice say-"That will catch up to you in Varanasi", which is where we were headed next.

At that moment I suddenly understood that life is like a river, and whatsoever we put into it, later on we draw the same thing out, be it love or hate.

I have certainly poured my share of stagnant or bitter water into the stream of life, which, I suppose, is unavoidable for someone corrupted by sin like I have been, but I have also attempted to will blessings and love out onto this agonizing realm, and I continue to try and domesticate the darkness within me so that this world can become filled with the love of which we are all worthy.

Either way, my *soror* and I left the peace of Rishikesh and made our way by train to the absolute unpeace of Varanasi, for there is no holy town on earth as unholy as Varanasi. Oh, it may receive its share of mystics, *sadhus*, and *muktas*, who gather about the shores of the Ganges in celebration of that sacred stream. But the town itself is the absolute shadow of all the light which is said to emanate from this holiest of Indian cities.

My *soror* and I were there for only a few days and that was a few too many. However, before we left, I still needed to reap, as it were, what I had sown back in Rishikesh, upstream in Varanasi.

The blessing I received in return for sending out the love vibe to the entire cosmos came in two installations.

The first installation came not in the horrid city of Vananasi itself- but in the nearby Buddhist town of Sarnath.

During our few days in Varanasi, my *soror* and I had considered taking a taxi to Sarnath, which lies some twenty kilometers north, but we had made no concrete plans. Then one night I had a dream in which I was drinking Chinese beer, and when I awoke I knew this had something to do with the Chinese 'spirit', as my dreams of booze always related to the spiritual realm and were therefore symbolic and not actual. However, I did not know what the dream portended until I awoke the next day and my *soror* and I decided we would take a journey to Sarnath that morning.

After hailing a taxi and surviving the punishing roads winding through and out of Varanasi, we arrived in Sarnath and found ourselves amidst a number of serene Buddhist temples, each built by followers of the dharma residing in other countries. There was a Sri Lankan Temple, a Tibetan Temple, a Japanese Temple, and, lo and behold, a Chinese Temple.

It was then that I realized the message of the dream- I was about to imbibe the Chinese Buddhist spirit.

I have said that the supreme emptiness which can be found in the temple in Dharamsala is a profound, liberating, and essential void. And I am full of gratitude for the privilege of having such an effortless benediction given to me. But now I was to realize another gift of a similar and yet wholly different nature altogether, which was also given to me without any effort or intent on my part. And that gift was stillness. Not emptiness, but absolute stillness. A stillness beyond words, beyond time, and beyond any experience or event known to the vicissitudes and caprices of human kind, for the stillness which exists in that Chinese Temple is unbelievable. It is indescribable. The stillness is a complete absence and yet an awareness of that absolute nothingness. And it is not a mental experience. It is holistic. The stillness which exists within the walls of the Chinese Buddhist Temple of Sarnath is a stillness which is ineffable, inimitable, and undeniable. Both my *soror* and I were so thoroughly embalmed in the stillness in which we bathed for perhaps thirty minutes while sitting in the lotus position, rapt in an inhuman calm, that when we eventually left the temple we knew we had experienced an unimaginable benediction, though we had no idea how it had come about, or what divine personage or force, or lack of force, or energy void, or what supernatural being had prepared that structure and placed their ubiquitous tranquility within its walls. We had no clue. To this day I have no idea who constructed it, or which Buddhist master poured his or her blessings and serenity into its hallowed sanctum, but I know that never before had I, nor have I since, experienced such a state of stillness as exists in that temple. It is a cosmic calm which cannot be aptly described, it can only be experienced, for it can only be *felt*.

Perhaps such unimaginable stillness has come from the Chinese nature described as *wei wu wei*- action without action- in which the individual exists in the untroubled, motionless realm of non-being, while yet operating within being. It is possible, because in the act of not-doing whatever an individual is doing- in that metaphysical contradiction where non-action is the epicenter of the action- a sublime vacuum of spirit is created, all unharmonious energies are sucked out in the evacuating whirlwind, and all that remains is the quiescent void.

I say this because having, in the past, been to the other side of doing, I have encountered the stillness of non-doing; I have stopped, completely stopped, even though I was still 'doing'. In this way I have 'stopped' through a subtle process of ambitionless, purposeless consciousness applied to all events in the realm of existence. In that unbound awareness the realm of being loosened its hold upon me, and I departed from the scene as I knew myself, and all that remained was the event that was happening effortlessly without me. And yet I was there. I was the non-doer *within* the doing, but I was not doing it.

I can understand, therefore, how such an ethereal black-hole can suck the crashing energies of the universe out of a certain area while an individual 'holds the space', as it is said. But I have no clue as to how that imperturbable void remains after the void-maker has vanished. I do not know. I doesn't matter. The stillness is, and is not. Amen.

*

eight

After that redemptive bath in the peace of the Chinese Buddhist Temple, we headed back to the bustle and unstillness of Varanasi, and the next day we boarded a train for Calcutta.

It was on this train, as we were leaving Varanasi, that the second installment of the blessing came to me.

As we chugged out of the city limits I fell into an inner calm and openness, and in that state I suddenly found myself in communion with God the Mother, and God the Father; I was in direct contact with them, and it seemed they had come to pay me a visit, in order to straighten a few things out for me.

I suppose this was necessary because at that time in my life I was still bound into an old way of thinking- the kind of thinking which defines things as good or bad, right or wrong. And due to such dualistic thinking I was often barraged by ideas of how to make life on earth better, of how to help others, and of why there was so much suffering in the world.

However, I was truly in for a divine teaching. For it was within the unexpected communion in which I was involved, while on the train, that I was unequivocally told by our divine Parents that everyone on earth was their child and that each person was receiving the guidance necessary for them at that time; the outer experiences of each individual may come as either gentle or harsh, but all outcomes were the actions of divine love. Therefore everything that happens to a person is an important lesson for their own journey towards wholeness. Everything is spiritually directed. Everything that comes and goes in anyone's life is part of their growth towards wholeness, no matter what. And since everyone who is here on earth has chosen to be here, and is receiving what they need to receive, there is no need to pity another, nor sympathize with their suffering. The essential thing is to have compassion without attachment.[18]

It was later pointed out to me that this realm has a long way to go before most individuals- most aspects of the whole- are evolved enough to become absolutely integrated into universal oneness. Many fragments have to grow a great deal more before they are ready for integration into wholeness. Therefore extreme patience is necessary.

This was an important earful for me to hear, because I am a tremendously impatient man. I am one who sees a goal and will not rest until it is accomplished. And since I can see the incredible state of unity possible for mankind, I want it to happen, now.

---

[18] Having said this, it is also important to help others when we are guided to do so, since we are all connected, and sometimes assistance is an essential component of our oneness. Therefore, discernment is necessary in order to know when one should leave another to the problems and agonies necessarily associated with his or her path, and when one should offer assistance because such help is divinely directed.

However, it was categorically told to me that at this time the patience of eternity is required, because the process of that commingling to oneness is a dexterous one, so as to not lose any of the derelict aspects of our wholeness along the way. To press forward too quickly is to injure the fragments building the whole. The cosmic cycle must run its course to completion. We must for now be at peace, and realize that everything is as it should be, and that the Great Mother and Father are looking out for all. Everything in due time. Patience and discernment are the requirements for now.[19]

This realm is a divine drama, designed, directed, and orchestrated by the combined will of the Mother and Father.

Our only task is to perfect ourselves, without inhibiting others, because our perfection will create the perfection of the whole. We need not worry over the suffering of the world, we need only send out our blessings knowing that to send blessings out to the entire world is to become the entire world, the *Mahayana*- the Greater Vehicle, and then to help steer that vessel home. *Om, baby!*

*

nine

After the blessing of communion, our train journey ended the next morning in Calcutta, where we intended only a brief stay, so as to visit one of the most important Goddess sites in all of India: the Kali Temple at Dakshineswar, a place made famous by

---

[19] A few experiments in biology have proven that all things must come to fruition in their right time: for example, it was shown that if a plant is briefly flashed with a grow-light in the middle of the night, the plant will believe morning has come, and will begin photosynthesizing at an improper time- when there is only darkness- thus entering an imbalance, and experiencing injury to its natural rhythm and growth.

Similarly, if a seed is uncovered just as it is sprouting, it will whither and die from an excess of light.

Furthermore, it is known that if a human opens a cocoon to help a butterfly get out, the butterfly will not be able to fly, because it is the struggle for liberation which gives the wings their strength. And so assistance in this case is actually detrimental.

the nineteenth century Hindu saint and devotee to the Mother, Sri Ramakrishna.

It is said that even as a boy Ramakrishna was given to bouts of mystic ecstasy. Though it was not until he was a young man and was hired as the keeper of the Kali Temple that he began, almost instantly, falling regularly into a deep, inexorable oblivion and *samadhi* while rapt in a catatonic union with the Divine Mother.

Apparently Ramakrishna soon became incapable of fulfilling his occupational duties, and it was only because of the temple manager's lucid understanding of the spiritual profundity of Ramakrishna's regress, that Ramakrishna was not sacked and sent out into the streets for his obvious incompetence; he was instead given a lifelong stipend, and a suspension of all duties, so that he could have his entire life free to perform the one essential task that he could not avoid performing anyways- communion with Her.

From that point onward Ramakrishna almost never left the temple grounds, and was so often found gripped in a spasmodic submersion with the Mother that he would go for days on end without moving or eating, and often would have to be mercilessly beaten by one of his 'devotees' in order to snap him away from the divine union long enough to force some rice down his throat so as to sustain him again during his exodus into the Goddess.

A few years later, Ramakrishna's wife- who had been married off to him as a young girl, as it sometimes happens in India- came to be with him at the temple. But Ramakrishna was now obviously incapable of being a husband, in the common sense, for he was inextricably married to Her, the Mother, and could not be expected to take on any semblance of a normal life. However, this wise woman by the name of Sarada Devi quickly recognized that what Ramakrishna had to offer was far greater than a comfortable home and a brood of children, and so she asked to remain with him at the temple, under his spiritual guidance, rather than return to the world in search of the profane accoutrements of life. In later years Ramakrishna was to proclaim that the three Goddess- Kali, Saraswati, and Laksmi- had become incarnate in the singular body of Sri Sarada Devi, and so the Mother whom he worshipped had become manifest right before him, as his wife, right in the temple grounds dedicated to Her being.[20]

My *soror* and I arrived at the temple complex on a rainy, monsoon afternoon. After following the trail of pilgrims up to the Kali image in the main building, we made our way into the adjacent, open-air meditation grounds, and sat down cross-legged amongst the supplicants.

Sitting side-by-side we both soon fell into a penetrating, meditative consciousness, and in that state I could feel my *soror's* soul become linked with the Mother's being, and a strong energy shift began pulling me into Her core.

I sensed then that physical gravity is simply a manifestation of the sublime gravitational pull the Mother has upon us, which draws us into Her, knowingly or not, in a subtle yet undeniable embrace that ends in either suffocation, or liberation. Suffocation if we do not love Her. Liberation if we do. As simple as that. However, the requirements of this love are perhaps different for every individual, since the Mother has a unique relationship with each of Her children.[21]

The most important requirement, of course, is to love Her *and* all Her children. However, this axiom does not imply that one must lie down and be walked upon by others. Oh no, we must remember- this is Kali. And the raging love of Kali does not ask for complacency. She asks for volatile, passionate, libertine love. In fact, it is Her demand for Her children's emancipation that causes Her to come with fire and force in order to drive Her children towards their own divine perfection. She is ruthless, and She is love, for She is ruthless love.

---

[20] This odd juxtaposition of a mystic's wife being also his mother is a common theme running through world mythology; it seems that at a certain point in the growth of the soul, the archetypical Mother manifests as a man's spouse; that is, his lover is an emanation of the Mother.

To encounter this, as I have encountered it, is to enter into an odd relationship with the archetypical blueprint of the cosmos. It means that now when you make love to your mate, you are making love to the Mother Goddess herself, who is your Mother, but is also your wife.

This is the reason why Jesus' mother and lover were both called Mary, for they were one being in two bodies; emanations of the same overself. The esoteric significance of their sameness is a sublime reality which a literal reading of the Bible does not betray.

[21] For example, at one point I received direct understanding that I would not have complete union with the Mother until I ceased to own a vehicle, because the Mother was not fond of the foul, polluting, desecrating act of oil production and consumption. And I can say that after I gave up owning a vehicle, my relationship with Her soon changed.

This raging love of the Mother reminds me of a certain species of owl in which the female, it is said, is a generous caregiver of her young until they are ready to spread their own wings. But when the fledglings have grown to the age when they must fly, She throws them out of the nest, sending them plummeting to the ground where the law of the jungle leaves only two options- fly, or die. And even when the soft-hearted father owl comes swooping down to aid and protect the young ones who have not yet risen in the wind, the mother owl comes tearing wildly out of the nest and drives him off, for She knows that love is not always about coddling and comfort; She knows that this world is a hard and unforgiving place, and the only way to give Her children a fighting chance is to be more hard and more unforgiving than the world.

This is Kali. This is Her love. Fly or die. She will not come to assist you. She is against you. And She is against you because She loves you. If you get sucked into Her gravity, into Her darkened soul, you will turn into ashes and vanish. And she will try to suck you in and hold you. She will pull you down into the pit of her black abyss, and She will close the door and devour you. And that is Her love. Because if you have not the strength to fly from Her bondage, you have not the right to fly. But if you love yourself enough to fight back, to grow and push and thrash and dance and scream and sing and fly, then alone will you have gleaned what Kali's dark, destructive love has to offer. Otherwise you are finished.

In that deep, gravitational pull I felt through my *soror's* soul and into Kali's gravity, I knew then that Her depth was so immense, so powerful, and so suffocating to anyone who had not yet learned how to fly, that I recoiled from the black hole of Her dark love, spread my wings, and looked towards the sky.

I had experienced too much expansion, too much liberation, too much disentanglement from the profane plane already, and had no desire to descend unwillingly into the claustrophobic matrix of the Goddess's womb.

Perhaps it was the case that it was Her love that was sucking me down, forcing me to grow strong enough to repel Her, but it was my intent that was lifting me from the ground, and I vowed that I would not go down.

I had just learned that I was no longer responsible for walking any one else's path. But to be sure I still had to walk my own. And my path was that of transcendence. I wanted freedom. I chose freedom. I chose to fly.[22]

*

ten

I chose to fly from the gravitational pull of that smothering Mother, and to ascend to the rarified Sky.

I swore allegiance to Krishna, to the limitless distance of liberation from this paradigm, and to the emancipation of my spirit from Her mighty talons.

I suppose it was this immense intent and determination of mine, as well as Krishna's benevolent descent upon my consciousness, which soon took me out and away farther than I could ever have imagined- for such a distance cannot be imagined, because it goes far beyond everything, including imagination.

This transcendent exodus began on the train as my *soror* and I departed Calcutta, while I was tearing myself away from the energetic constraints of the dark Mother, heading south towards a mountain renowned for its cosmic communion with the ever-free Father- Mt. Arunachala.

On that train ride I slowly but undeniably became untangled from the Mother's clutches, and therefore became assimilated into absolute, liberation consciousness. At least this is what I called it at first, for I had never experienced such a tremendous release from all that is.

I had floated out of this paradigm, out of humanity, out of the world, and had entered a subtle consciousness which goes far beyond anything that exists. Anything. For there is nothing which exists which is as subtle as this non-existent, liberated

---

[22] The reader might wonder- how is it possible to have had such intimate communion with the Mother and Father one minute, and then such repulsion the next? The reason is this: all of life is a contradiction, a duality, including the Godhead. There are light and dark aspects to both the Father and the Mother. Both are necessary. Destruction is as essential as creation. However, given that we all have free-will, we have the right and the ability to choose our own directions, our own alliances, and our own responses to this dual nature of the Godhead.

consciousness. It is pure awareness, nothing more, and it is not bound by anything within this realm or any other.

I had been taken across the great divide by Krishna himself. I had received the benediction of transcendental consciousness. I was now outside of all that is, was, or will be. I was free.

It was an incredible experience to receive this initiation while humming southward on a crammed and noisy Indian train. It was truly incredible to be a part of such a profane, involved, manifested milieu which existed on that train, and yet to be totally apart from it as well. I had entered the subtle realm of eternal, transcendental awareness, and suddenly all the words that I had read years earlier in the *Bhagavad Gita*, and the *Uddhava Gita*- in which Krishna expounds the actuality of this transcendent realm, which is beyond everything that exists, no matter what- made sense, and I realized that I had arrived in the unbound place of which he was talking.

I knew then that in order to get there you have to take all things that exist in any realm, visible or invisible, physical or metaphysical, obvious or obscure, material or mental, and, enclosing them into a singular event, step outside of that event altogether; in doing so you become the subtle, transcendent consciousness which lies outside of the one event of all that is. You have to let go of everything to go beyond everything. This is detached peace.

Nothing but conscious clear space and peace lies beyond all realms, beyond all ideas and understandings, beyond self and source, beyond being and non-being, for beyond everything is the realm of eternal, transcendent consciousness.

To enter transcendental consciousness is to become the tranquil, reactionless space. To get to that liberated space you cannot associate yourself with the plane of manifestation, nor with the mind, nor with any spirit of force, no matter what, for liberation consciousness is not in any way related to worldly or even otherworldly actions or non-actions; it is *absolutely* independent of all realms.

Whereas this plane embodies all dualities that are yet one- the invisible and visible, male and female, good and evil, etcetera- transcendental consciousness is beyond all duality, and cannot be compared, or related to anything, however sacred or profane.

Neither can transcendental consciousness be apprehended by the senses nor the mind, for it is absolute, inviolable, effortless, identitiless awareness.

In order to get there, as I have said, you have to let go of everything. You have to let all of manifestation be, and you have to penetrate through and beyond it, for transcendental consciousness is far more subtle than any form of manifestation or thought. Beyond self and source lies this liberated, eternal awareness.

This liberation is different than enlightenment, because enlightenment is caught up in the idea of wisdom, of understanding; but with the attainment of liberating, transcendental consciousness you don't necessarily understand anything, and yet you are *free*.

Transcendental consciousness *is* peace, and is a peace unlike any peace in the relative field, for it is not associated with nor mirrored by unpeace. Transcendental peace is absent of all qualities; it is a nothingness that yet *is*.

This is the realm of unity, of oneness, which is beyond anything that is composed of definition, duality, or opposition.

The mind and the eyes inherently divide and fragment the world which lies before us, and therefore cannot be used as tools to realize the One. The One, subtle, eternal, transcendental consciousness lies neither within nor without. It is apprehended only when anything that can be thought of or experienced is released.

As the self emerges out of form, out of the duality of existence and non-existence, of life and death, it enters the timeless space of eternity.

I look back now on earlier years along my path, and see how this transcendental consciousness was attempting to come through to my awareness by penetrating the thick cloud of my unwitting dilemmas.

In fact, as a young man I would often 'liberate' my paradigmatic consciousness by inwardly acknowledging to myself a de-affirmation of this human paradigm; I would do this through a subtle method, by consciously perceiving that reality is *"not-I*, and, *not-this*".

Although I never experienced anything, at that time, like I was experiencing now, somewhere in the dark recesses of my eternity I knew that I had to go beyond everything in order to be aware of my true, subtle, immortal nature.

Krishna had granted me an immense boon by assisting my attainment of transcendental consciousness. And yet, perhaps I was destined to arrive at this liberating awareness at some point anyway, because I had often categorically stated many times in the past that I did not want to come back to this plane nor this paradigm, ever again. I had become incredibly discontented and bored with the whole mad show, and I wanted to be done with it once and for all. I wanted to leap off of the cyclic wheel of becoming, only I did not know how. But now it had happened. I had become liberated through my blind ambition not to be sucked back into the dark Mother's great gravity. Krishna had heard my call, and had carried me into the vast reaches of the eternal void of awareness. I had attained eternal, omnipresent, transcendental consciousness.[23]

To become eternal is to awaken to that which is beyond anything bound to time. To go beyond time is to go beyond becoming. To go beyond becoming is to *be*, but not in the sense of anything that has a being, for this eternity is a subtle awareness which ought never be compared nor confused with any partiality, any thing, or any event. Only the negation of all that is will offer a glimpse of that which cannot be negated.

*

eleven

The subtle, transcendental awareness is so fragile when it is first encountered that any effortful action which is done in relation to the temporal realm will quickly pull the individual's consciousness back down into this human paradigm.

---

[23] In fact, I had unconsciously documented the growing seed of this subtle, transcendental consciousness in some of the art pieces I had produced over the years. My mandala *The Tree of Life*, shown at the beginning of this book, is a perfect example; I now know that the two eyes present in behind the main design represent the subtle, eternal, unbound awareness of which I am speaking. Many of my earlier drawings contained such eyes, though I had no clue that these were subconsciously representing the subtle awareness that is beyond all form and thought.

I was pulled back down. Down I came, down into this universe, down into this galaxy, down into our solar system, down to earth, down, down, farther down, back into India, into the train, and back into the bustle of this human plane.

After a brief stop in Madras, my *soror* and I headed for Mt. Arunachala- the destination which had provoked the entire spectacular pilgrimage which we were now temporally experiencing.

I say that Mt. Arunachala was the original goal of our journey because our whole trip had been motivated not only by an inner hunger to return to India, but also by an intensely focused dream which I had perhaps six months earlier. In the dream I was shown an overhead view of the map of India, and then a hand moved across the map, charting a similar course to the one which we had just taken over the last month. Then, with unquestionably deliberate intent, a finger from the hand pointed directly at the place on the map where Mt. Arunachala stands, and a small circle was drawn around the area. I awoke and knew that the guidance had been given, and I would follow.

Upon arriving in Tiruvannamalai, the horrid little town at the foot of the holy Mt. Arunachala, my *soror* and I booked into a hotel and then went out for an initial wander through the streets and alleyways nearby. As such I soon began to lose more touch with the great distance of the subtle transcendental consciousness which had so profoundly opened up in me on the train earlier. I was immersed in action, and so had been pulled away from the eternal non-action.

I realize now why Krishna was ever exhorting Arjuna to "give up the fruits of the action", because to give up the fruits of action is to release all outcome, expectation, and passionate attachment to anything that is happening, and so to remain in the distant, detached, transcendent state. Without such surrender of the fruits, one remains bound energetically into the goals and parameters of the paradigm and therefore can no longer transcend beyond it.

Only after giving up the fruits of all action can one be intimate with the transcendent, effortless non-doer, while acting as the involved, effortful doer. Only by not caring about the ephemeral, can one enter into the eternal.

Nevertheless, I was still chasing the fruit, and was back in the non-eternal paradigm, and so we spent a few days recuperating from the two-day train journey which had brought us south, and wandered aimlessly around and through the pollution and ugliness which chronically pervades every Indian town and city. However, although the main streets of Tiruvannamalai were no less grotesque than any other in the country, once we were off of the major thoroughfares there was a peaceful and pristine community to be found.

An amazing aspect of such areas of Tiruvannamalai, as in other southern Indian villages, is the ubiquitous chalk mandalas drawn on the ground in front of each house every morning.

The mandala is a circular symbol of wholeness, and the variety and artistry contained in the numerous mandalas drawn throughout the backstreets of the town were splendid, living signs of the sacred wholeness of the mountain itself, and indeed the eternal soul within us all.

Rising above those chalk mandalas is Mt. Arunachala, a divine and mythical protrusion emerging out of the rocky and dry land of Tamil Nadu. It is said to be a giant lingam, caused by Shiva's descent onto the earth at that very spot. And, to be sure, it is a geophysical wonder which exudes a cosmic peace not unlike the Ganges at Rishikesh.[24]

It was upon the slopes of this mythical mountain that Ramana Maharishi, the divine Hindu master of the twentieth century, spent his entire adulthood, and remained there, often in retreat for years on end, deep in contemplation in one of the unique cave houses that exist on the mountain for that very purpose.

After two days of rest my *soror* and I took a rickshaw across town to visit the ashram created by Ramana, and there we found an immense crowd gathered for the centenary celebration of his birth. We had no prior knowledge this gathering was to happen

---

[24] Furthermore, when viewed from a specific angle, the entire mountain appears like a pyramid, and one of its outcroppings looks uncannily like a Sphinx. I had seen a similar natural phenomenon many years earlier, while camping for a week at Wharariki Beach, which lies on the west coast of the south island of New Zealand.

After making these odd connections, and sharing them with my *soror*, she then remembered a dream in which she had been shown a mountain that was a pyramid which was both natural and manmade, and she was told in the dream that this was Mt. Arunachala.

I wonder, therefore, if the pyramid builders in ancient Egypt, as well as the Mayan and Inca architects in Central and South America, who designed similar man-made structures, were psychically picking up on a cosmic, archetypical pattern which somehow focuses the spirit onto the earth, thus creating an epicenter connecting heavenly processes to earth.

and we took the synchronicity as a serendipitous sign. And no doubt it was, for I had come to the area to experience Mt. Arunachala alone, and had never read anything by Ramana Maharishi, nor knew much about his life and teachings. Nor did I know what effect his living spirit would have upon me during the days which followed. But that effect would soon become apparent.

My *soror* and I mingled through the Indian crowd for a bit, strolled around the ashram grounds, and then made our way into the main meditation hall where we found an empty spot amongst the pilgrims and supplicants, and sat down in silence.

Almost instantly I fell into communion with Ramana Maharishi's spirit. In that deep connection he and I began a subtle conversation on aspects of the spiritual life, during which I was given understandings on the nature of the role of the spiritual mentor in the world, and the ways in which the spirit can be exercised amidst humanity.

One thing we discussed was the peril of being too open to the chaos and karma of others in one's vicinity. This was an important topic to cover, because out of their love for all agonizing humanity around them, both Ramana Maharishi and Ramakrishna had died at about the age of sixty from cancer; they had taken on the clogged spirits of those around them, and had thus been clogged by the overwhelming amount of dis-ease within humanity. Both of these great men could have lived on much longer by avoiding intimacy and contact with those who came to them for guidance and succor, but in the end neither of them could turn their love away from their fellow man; they died willingly, out of love.

I honor the decisions these two immortal souls made, and the compassion and courage which spurned them to give up their own lives for the benefit of others. If there is such a thing as sacrifice on earth, then these two have accomplished it. However, I have grown into a different temperament, for I was also born with a very open spirit, and have suffered over the years in my own way from such a defenseless disposition. But after becoming aware of the perils of such openness in my early thirties, I struggled to close that chasm within myself, and to prevent others from penetrating my defenses and sending their troubled energy into me.

Therefore, during my subtle discussion with Ramana Maharishi, I communicated my sense of the dangers of such openness, and admitted that I for one had no desire, even if out of compassion, to take on too much of mankind's pathos, and declared to Ramana that I would prefer to express blessings *out* into others, as I had done in Rishikesh, rather than receive unconscious unblessings from them.

I recognized that Ramana understood my position and seemed to consider my intent correct for my spirit and disposition. At least he did not consider me a coward or a knave, because after this communion I would encounter his spirit twice more, in still more profound and direct interactions than I had on this privileged day.

These two episodes came about a few days later, as my *soror* and I made our way up the winding, cobbled path which begins behind the ashram, and weaves its way up the mountain towards the cave houses in which Ramana Maharishi spent many years in solitude and silence. It is within these sacred enclaves that his immortal spirit is completely present and available. And it is here that I received his great and benevolent teachings.

Upon arriving on our first visit to the cave house, my *soror* and I took up meditative positions inside one of the inner chambers, and the communion began.

What I learned that day was something I had always known but which had never before crystallized within me with the certitude I now felt while in communion with Ramana's consciousness.

What I realized was that the self in everyone is the same self, and that in loving others we love our own self, and in hating others we hate our own self also. It is the subtle nature of this undivided oneness which must be awoken in order to remove the separative consciousness which divides us from each other, and therefore from our greater selves.

I understood clearly that every I is the same I; that every I is one I. My I and your I are the same I. Many forms veil the formless I, but we are all the same I. And that is why we all call ourselves I.

All judgment ends, all hatred ends, all division ends when every I is known as one I.

And since every I is the same I, there is no individual I, only everything. One. For the self is everyone, but no single individual, and the self is everything, but no single thing.

Within such mystical oneness, there is no such duality as me and you. Only I. There is no such duality as us and them. Only I. I am I. You are I. We are I. One I. The same I. I to I. One I.

Without knowing and feeling this underlying unity, all suffering, war, and despair will continue.

But when each I is known as every I, then there is no separation, no judgment, no hatred, but only I, one I, which is love. For love is the absence of separation, the absence of division, and the absence of 'other'. In love, I *is* every I. One I. I.

This was an incredible teaching on the nature of oneness. After my *soror* and I left the cave house that day I felt immense gratitude and well-being, knowing that I had just received perhaps the most important lesson there is to receive in this human realm.

But to be sure I was in for another lesson, one which would force me to abort any idea of separation or duality altogether. This time, though, it would not come from the blessed countenance of Ramana Maharishi, it would come from the Dark Goddess herself. Amen.

*

Part III
THE UNION OF SPIRIT AND FLESH

"Primus homo de terra terranus. Secundus homo caelo caelestis."
(First, man of the earth, terrestrial. Second, man of the sky, celestial.)
Corinthians I, 15:47

one

There is a fallow upheaval awakening from its dormant sleep, a raging blossom of love and unity rising out of our howling souls towards each other.

There is an apocalyptic disentangling, a galactic renovation, a novel fusion re-creating our abandoned home.

Our lives are ephemeral bridges between the eternal spirit above, and the eternal soul below. I know that, for I have learned.

My lesson came on the shores of the tropical paradise of Goa, where my *soror* and I had retreated as an escape from the turmoil and tension of India proper. And what an escape it was, for to enter Goa is to leave India.

We had left India, but during our exodus to the west coast of Goa I had regained the liberating effects of transcendental consciousness. And so I was once again floating in that removed state of non-being as we came upon the glorious sands of being. I had once again gone beyond the troubles and confusions of this world, beyond the attachment and the revulsion, beyond need and fulfillment, beyond worry and woe. I had grabbed hold of the sky once again, and this time I would not let go and come down.

I believed then that through the guidance of Christ and the assistance of Krishna, having crossed over to the shore of transcendental consciousness, and thus liberated from the bondage of this realm of birth and death, I would help others achieve the same, if they so desired. But, as I said, I was in for a lesson; I was soon to realize that to attain transcendental consciousness is to have attained an immensely important, incredibly subtle and profound aspect of the eternal nature of existence, but it is only one half of the coin, and without the other half, such remote and empyrean awareness is but the false redemption of a person sitting in a movie theater and feeling at peace because they are not part of the action.

This is a conclusion which only the mind could arrive at. For the person, sitting in the theater, watching a movie in which they play no part, is still a person in the theater, and therefore remains as part of the greater play of existence- the part that is the body.

Given that, my *soror* and I arrived in a small beach-side hamlet on the coast of Goa late one evening, where we settled into a pleasant little bungalow, and, after completing the minimal tasks required to feel at home, we fell into the gentle rhythm that is easily attainable in such seaside destinations.

As such I continued to be in the great abyss of transcendental consciousness, and therefore remained in a liberated awareness, freed from the paradigm of this world and humanity. However, I had forgotten that my body remained behind to take part in life as it exists on this great Mother Earth.

I had gone to the extreme of transcendental consciousness, to the zenith of the great liberated space which is outside of everything associated with this realm, and what happened is... I got burned. Badly burned. Literally.

This came the day after our arrival in Goa. We had gone down to the beach, laid out our giant sarong, and settled down to bask in the sun. I sat there in the serenity of liberation and detachment from this realm, and in that distant realm of consciousness I lost body consciousness and within an incredibly brief period I received the worst sunburn I have ever experienced. I got burned, burned like I had never been burned before. Parts of my body were so badly torched that I received almost second degree burns. I was aghast. I had only been out a couple of hours, the same as my *soror*, who had suffered none of the calamity which had now overtaken me.

The next few nights were a fit of agony and discomfort the likes of which I had never experienced before. I could not believe that I had received that level of a scalding in such a short time. But the reason for this was not simply a lack of recognition of the sun's power, it was a disregard for the consciousness of the body, and of all matter, for that matter.

I came to this understanding on the second night of my writhing and pain. In one of the brief periods in which I had fallen into a disquieted sleep during that night, I had a quick visitation from the Goddess herself, and in that brief visit She stated one thing, and one thing only; with matter-of-fact, compassionate wisdom, She declared: "The flesh is Divine." And then She departed, and I awoke, and understood immediately how my partisanship to the subtle, transcendental consciousness had created a massive imbalance, and the other half of my being- my flesh side- had screamed back at me with a ruthless howl the likes of which I will never forget.[25]

Even today, when I enter into that great space which transcends this realm altogether, I can feel a tingling sensation in the exact same places where I had been so badly scorched. For consciousness, the spirit, and the flesh are intimately connected, and what happened to my flesh in Goa was a direct result of my consciousness departing from it.

I now proclaim unabashedly that this divinity of the flesh, and of all matter, is absolute. This is a reality which I had understood in the past, but the draw of liberation through the incredible release of transcendental consciousness had overtaken me, and I had left this realm like that man who watches a movie in the theater and is glad to not be a part in the action. But in fact I had not left the action of this realm, only my consciousness had left, while my body remained behind to deal with the departure.

As I have said, I had already known and experienced the absoluteness of the flesh and all matter many times, but at the zenith of liberation consciousness such things are all too easily forgotten or obscured. This is why so many things in this world become lopsided, and run counter to the needs of the flesh, the earth, and the soul, all of which are the same one thing.

The thrill of the freedom of transcendental consciousness, of being liberated from a realm in which I had flailed and struggled for so long, was such a relief and an inviting sanctuary that I was drawn like Icarus to the sun, forgetting that I was made of substance, and that the great distance I had achieved was worth nothing without a similarly profound closeness.

I had not yet merged the transcendent *with* the immanent; I had not yet blended the two into one. When I had rejected the Mother's gravity back in the Kali Temple, I had created a chasm which I now had to bridge once again, for I had thought it important to escape the Mother, and it is. But I did not know that

---

[25] "O Mother of the worlds!
Those who have reached that birth amongst men
Which is so difficult to attain,
And in that birth their full faculties,
Yet nathless do not worship Thee,
Such, though having ascended to the top of the stairs,
Nevertheless fall down again."
 Bhuvanes'vari (from the *Tantrasara*, quoted by Sir John Woodroffe in *Hymns to the Goddess and Hymn to Kali*. Ganesh and Company, Madras. 2001, p 33,34)

in the love bridge between spirit and flesh, you cannot escape from Her, you can only escape *with* Her.

Only the mind divorced from the body could imagine such a necessary union as inessential. Only the mind divorced from the body can create wild fantasies about how things could or should be. But only the body can say how things *are*. For the mind divorced from the body says "I am right and they are wrong"; but the body says "there is no 'they'", for all flesh is one flesh. The mind divorced from the body says "you should do this, and you shouldn't do that"; but the body says "there are no shoulds", there is only the organic rhythm of *natural* being. The mind divorced from the body says "this is good, and that is bad"; but the body says "there is no such duality", there only *is*, and that isness is one. The mind divorced from the body says "do this, do that, run here, run there, learn, and strive, and despair, and consume, and discard, and work, and wake, and see the clock, and watch the clock, and die by the clock", and the body says "Fuck you!"

There is a great difference between belief and actuality. Actuality *is*. Belief is a matrix laid over the actuality, modifying it experientially to coincide with the belief system of the individual without affecting the substratum of actuality. The important thing is to rid consciousness of all preconceptions and 'ideas', and cause it to descend into the actuality of *isness*, so as to experience the true nature of matter. Therefore consciousness must grow *with* being, in union, rather than as a spotlight projected onto the scene from above. Otherwise, from such a removed height, consciousness takes on no substantial, actual part, but only propagates an eternal non-reality- a 'play' which denies the reality of its actors.

To bring consciousness down into the reality of this realm, is to draw the spirit into the flesh.

And it is not until the complete union of transcendental consciousness *with* the immanent, feeling soul occurs, that the eternal, whole self is truly 'liberated' from the confines of this realm. This new unity includes not only the subtle, transcendental consciousness permeating all that is, but also the gross, immanent being that is all that *is*.

The mind may know what is illusion, but the body knows what is real. The mind may know how to think, but the body knows how to *feel*.

To feel is to enter the domain of the absolute. To feel is to enter the flesh, to expand the heart, and so to enter into union with all other life.

To feel is to become one with the Goddess, which is to become the All.

After one awakens to the detached, transcendental consciousness, one must then also awaken to the intimate, immanent soul of matter (*anima mundi*). For then, through the dissolution of separative identity, one becomes the macrocosmic *yin* and *yang*, the entirety of the Self *and* Soul, male *and* female, consciousness and matter, spirit and flesh.

And to combine such polarities is to become the embodiment of the Great Cosmic Father, and Great Cosmic Mother, which is to *become* Avalon. *Om, baby!*

*

two

I maintain that the great emancipation arrived at, through transcendental consciousness, is an immensely important, immensely subtle aspect of the eternal nature of the self. But I also maintain now that the divinity and immortality of the flesh is equally as important. Yin is nothing without yang, spirit is nothing without flesh.

Again, to attain transcendental consciousness and to then believe with relief that one has been liberated 'out' of the parameters of the flesh is a false conclusion that only the mind divorced from the body and heart can accept. This is because the soul- of the pseudo-free individual who has attained transcendental consciousness- remains a reality, and remains trapped in matter, and is now hopelessly lost from the spirit, which has unwittingly floated away from life by believing that all, including the soul, is nothing but a fantasy.

The problem is that consciousness can perceive and know all that is, but it cannot *feel*, for feeling is a function of the body and soul. And so when the spirit has flushed the whole human drama and flesh down the cosmic toilet, by assuming it all to be a dirty illusion, the soul gets thrown out as well.

Fortunately this abandonment of the soul is actually an impossibility- for the spirit and soul are linked eternally, and inextricably. And the agony of this massive separation, felt completely by the flesh and soul, will eventually draw the hovering spirit back down into matter to retrieve Her, be it in this incarnation, or in a future embodiment. The agony of separation will not go away, for flesh, like spirit, is also eternal, even though its form changes shape eternally; the absoluteness and eternity of form is not to be found in the variety of 'forms' which matter takes, but in the immortal soul of matter itself.

Transcendental consciousness is therefore not about leaving this realm, but about awakening to the aspect of the eternal Self which is not bound to this realm, though it entirely permeates this realm. This is the consciousness which Christ stated was "In, but not of" this world.

There is also, however, a thoroughly immanent, eternal consciousness, which is 'in and of' this world, and therefore is bound to this realm- though not in the same way the suffering, misperceiving, unawakened self is bound; the immanent soul is bound to this realm because it *is* this realm- it *is* the consciousness of matter.

This immanence is the eternal yin, whereas transcendental consciousness is the eternal yang, both of which are essential polarities producing wholeness. We must be 'in, but not of', and we must also be 'in *and* of'.

Whereas transcendental consciousness is entirely free from all constraints and characteristics, and is therefore an incredibly important consciousness into which we should awaken, an important *caveat* remains: that is- transcendental consciousness *transcends* the duality and limitations of *this* realm, but it still remains only one half of the great cosmic duality, of which immanence is its counterpart. Therefore, during the pursuit of, and after the awakening to transcendental consciousness, the liberated individual must not fall under the delusion that life is an 'illusion', as many historical mystics and current spiritual books suggest. For it is only in balancing out the yang- transcendental consciousness- with the yin- immanent matter-consciousness- that one attains to true wholeness, and therefore becomes a living aspect of the Tree of Life, uniting heaven and earth.

Thus it is always important to remember that no matter what degree of cosmic consciousness, freed indisputably from the human paradigm, we have attained, the flesh, the earth, and all matter are yet divine, and need to be attended to, intimately embraced, and acknowledged as part of the whole self. The mind must permeate through and enter the viscera, because Her is *here*.

To retrieve Her, the soul, out of the confines of matter, to make Her smothered voice a song, to lift Her up into freedom, is to turn away from the outward show, and to turn within to Her home.

Without this metaphysical grounding in the physical, the awakening to transcendental consciousness will only lead to an existential abandonment of life, of the inner soul, and thus will have as much functional value as a kite without a string. The spirit will become derelict in the cosmos.

To operate in this realm is to accept this realm, to truly and fully *be* this realm, which is to be *real*. In and of.

The serpent needs wings as the wings need the serpent. The flesh needs the spirit, as the spirit needs the flesh.[26]

Immanence is as essential as transcendence.

We must be in this realm *and* beyond it. In, and of, and not-of. Immanent *and* transcendent. Relative *and* absolute. Consciousness *and* matter. Spirit *and* flesh. *Om, baby!*

*

three

As I have said, consciousness may exist eternally, but being also exists eternally, though its form ever changes. To love *being* is to cause the flesh to dissolve into the boundaryless oneness of mystic matter. In this way substance is what connects the spirit to the soul. Substance is the bridal chamber within which these two eternities are wedded and consummate the Eucharistic marriage of the spirit and soul which is flesh.

---

[26] When Christ called himself the Son of Man, was he not therefore calling himself a child of the earth? For the first man was Adam, a name which means 'the red earth'.
    After all, the word 'human' comes from the Latin word *homo*, which comes originally from *humus*, the soil. We are of the earth, as was our first ancestor, Adam. We need to admit, accept, and embrace this.

When consciousness enters matter- when spirit enters flesh- that consciousness will only feel confined if it misperceives the flesh as a specific 'part' of the all, rather than recognizing that all matter is one great, cosmic whole. When matter is experienced as vast as is consciousness, there is no sense of limitation, only an immense, glorious union of the King and Queen, within the now limitless individual; matter is not limiting unless you think that you are *only* a specific part of matter.

By entering into matter we expand it; when consciousness descends into form, form itself becomes unlimited, and grows to meet consciousness in the dual dance of ecstatic oneness.

Thus the form must be hallowed as form, and the space must be hallowed as space, because both consciousness and form are immortal. These are separated until they are united within us.

To be the immortal, transcendent, all-pervading male spirit, *and* the immortal, immanent, all-pervading female soul, is to be the subtle, invisible androgynous 'I' which lives above, behind, and within all existence and experience.

Emerging from our room in Goa the next morning, after awakening to my abandonment of the flesh, I noticed that someone had hung a large beach towel on a clothes-line just outside of our door, and on it there was the design of the union of the sun and moon- the marriage of Sol and Luna. This is a symbol used in alchemy for wholeness- for macrocosmic androgyny, where the union of the Father and Mother occurs *within* the individual.[27]

Later that day I did something I had never done before- I mixed a cocktail of red wine and white port- symbolizing the convergence of the Father and Mother- and drank down the slurry in honor of their blessed union within me.

Merging the female into the male, one becomes another archetype altogether- the *sacred androgyne*- which is pure male

---

[27] To unite the spirit with the flesh is the essential intent behind Patanjali's *Yoga Sutras*- in which he continually suggests that consciousness must be held in the body. This is also the intent behind the Catholic Eucharist, in which the body, symbolized as the bread, is united with the spirit, symbolized in the wine; flesh and spirit become one- the body and the blood.

As well, the great Tibetan Buddhist mantra, *om mani padme hum*, implores the same event, beginning with *om*, the great, cosmic vibration, and finishing with *hum*, the manifestation of that macrocosmic perfection within the actual, which is the union of spirit and flesh.

consciousness and pure female energy, united in an inward marriage dance that is itself a microcosmic mirror of the cosmic union danced throughout this unwitting world.

When this union occurs within us we are no longer foreigners within matter; we are no longer non-being confused by the event of being. Where once we declared ourselves to be 'in, but not of', now we experience the marriage within ourselves of male and female, spirit and soul, consciousness and isness. Now we are 'in, and of'.

As the light from the sun coming through a magnifying glass, though transfigured, is still the light from the sun, though now with focused intention, I became absolutely physical, absolutely of this paradigm; infinity focused *as* this specific existence.

By accepting myself *as* matter, I found my soul within matter, and then matter opened up into a great space wherein there lies a boundaryless intimacy with all things.[28]

By focusing on the Mother and Father in union *within* me, I became a temple of the divine whole.

When a person takes on the flesh and becomes one with all matter, he or she integrates the outer spirit with the inner soul, and adds the frequency of matter to the frequency of mind, which together create a whole new, subtle harmony. Now that person is not only outside of existence looking in- as the male spirit naturally is- he or she is also 'in and of' matter, which the female soul naturally is. The individual has become a new person, now a living bridge between two separate eternities- spirit and flesh.

This all-pervasive consciousness/being is the union of the eternal Female with the eternal Male, and this union is the subtle Self which is both transcendent *and* immanent, in that it pervades all, yet is not bound at all.

To become the one all-pervading consciousness is one thing, to become the one all-pervading matter is another. To be both, and to make those two macrocosmic eternities into a singular event, is another commingling altogether. These are the stages of cosmic unity, wherein matter and consciousness, spirit and flesh, and form and formlessness become the same great subtle sea in, and through, and of which the now liberated 'self' awakens in, and

---

[28] "It is the origin of All, the consecration of the Universe; its inherent strength is perfected, if it is turned into Earth." Hermes Trismegistus (third rubric of *The Emerald Tablet*)

of, and as, the one event of which it is, but is not bound by that which it is. *Om, baby!*

*

four

Having finally connected the transcendental, Father spirit, with the immanent, Mother soul, during our stay in Goa, I dreamt a dream one night in which I was told that I was "helping Narayana."

I awoke and was somewhat befuddled, as I had no prior knowledge of that name. Soon enough, however, I learned from a book on Hindu mythology that Narayana is an uncommon name for Vishnu, but was originally a pseudonym for Brahma. Therefore I realized I was being told that my self was casting light on the Self; that is, I was helping God the Father become intimate with God the Mother.[29]

From this experience, as well as other supporting intuitions and dreams from my past, I know that the microcosmic self is an essential component to the cosmic control of this realm. And by that I mean that humans are not mere recipients of divine design and decree, we are also necessary, integral, valuable and powerful aspects of the whole. In this sense every individual has a voice and power to shift the entire universe, for God requires man in order to understand and modify the nature of *being*.[30]

As aspects of the God and Goddess, we are intimately connected with the whole. There is no division. If we scream in anguish, our Godselves hear us. If we raise a cheer, our Godselves rejoice. If we give thanks, or Godselves are humbled.

Individuality *and* universality are essential; the leaf is the tree is the leaf; everything is of the same whole, but that whole is made healthy through differentiation. This is the ecology of spirit,

---

[29] In a similar and yet reverse way, I say that Christ prayed only to the Father, and not to the Mother, *because* he was already with the Mother; he was already an incarnate, fleshy, human, feeling being. He was already one with the Mother. All that was left was to become one with the Father. And this is what he prayed for, attained, and spoke about.

[30] It was partly for this reason that Christ descended into this world- so as to apotheosize mankind's role in the cosmos.

wherein due to the interdependence of all beings, the greater the diversity of individuals, the greater is the strength of the whole.

I know now that God must *assume* my experience in the assumption of my self, just as I assume God's in the descent of the Self, for we are one. I am God experiencing my creation. I have survived the perilous descent into flesh, and now am like a distant colonialist with a direct phone-line to the monarchy.

But don't get the idea that the dominoes of wholeness fell in perfect pattern right out before me, nor that things went smoothly and in harmony for me. I have attempted to relate the glories and gore as they persisted side by side for me.

Things rarely go smoothly on this plane. There is always a push, and a push back. And though I was often at peace and accepting of the generous guidance I was given, I was at times equally discontented and enraged. And yet I do not count these supposed lesser human qualities as negative, for to block the flow of emotions is to inhibit the motions coming to and through you. In fact, at times rage is more divine than acquiescence, and confusion more appropriate than certitude.

It is hard not to be dissatisfied. I should know, for I have attained immortality, and still I am dissatisfied. However, to realize this lack of satisfaction, built into the human disposition, is to come to a certain type of peace. Not the peace of the transcendent Self, but rather a human peace; a limited peace that is a consolation in a sea of human unpeace.

I say therefore, in humility, that if at times I engaged selflessly in service to the greater cause, I also turned often enough with great frustration against the light, and pushed forward towards my own soul's needs, with more than a little might. But in the end I realized that God needs this form of creative rebellion, for we are the ones in the living *now* of life, and only in true response and true expression of our true feelings do we convey the reality of this realm to the consciousness of God, the Father, and to the soul of God, the Mother. Only in loving our inner souls do we mature in our relationship with our divine parents. Only when we love ourselves can we truly love God.

If my spirit and soul raged or rebelled against God, it was only so that I could become more like God, and therefore become one with God, for God is neither dependent nor independent, God is an interdependent One. In order for God to be all, all must have the courage to be God. Unity *is* diversity.

Thus it is healthy to rebel against God, for God learns through us also. We expand God by becoming God, not by laying down in lazy surrender. In becoming God we add to God, we do not divide God. Pour a bucket of water into the ocean, and the ocean remains a great sea, only now it is one bucket larger. This is true devotion: to become ourselves so completely, so guiltlessly- even if it means rebelling and raging against God- that in our wholeness we become God, and so add to the God we had just rejected.

This is the fire by which the blade is forged, the struggle from which the muscle grows strong, the poison which is also the cure. At times, to stand against God is to become one with God, as Saul turned St. Paul proved to us many centuries ago.

Only that which stands apart from God creates a shadow; the sun radiates only light, and only that which detaches from the sun becomes an 'object' which creates a shadow.

However, to become separate from God- to create a shadow- and then to re-integrate that separateness and shadow back into God, is to expand the Godhead beyond its original radiance.

Thus Lucifer- the light bearer- who has fallen away from God, is then reintegrated back into the One.

The light pours into us from outside. The dark pushes out of us from within. But as we deny ourselves and allow only the outside light to push its way in, and do not allow the dark within to push its way out, whatever is inside of us becomes repressed, ugly, and angry.

It is only when we honor our inner beings- the dark, mysterious self behind the eyes- and push back against the external, that we develop a sacred space within ourselves, and attain to a great inner emptiness and peace.

The parts deny the whole, the parts rebel against the whole, and yet the parts fulfill the whole.

This is unity in diversity. This is individuation *and* union; to merge oneself into the all, become all, and yet remain distinct enough to be individual- an integrated aspect of the whole, an eternal part of the eternal whole, a unique self in a sea of Self, an immortal, inviolable, recognizable pattern in the carpet of the cosmos.

To become such is to be like an eternal rock in the ephemeral river of life.

This is the *solve et coagula* stage of alchemy, wherein the macrocosmic, ethereal self condenses into the diamond body, and one becomes individually 'established' in eternity.

To get to the inviolable distillate of the subtle self, and then condense it down into a novel eternity, is indeed like smelting invisible gold out of gross ore; to do so is to crystallize the invisible God within, out of the grosser apparitions, and so to become an actualized, separate eternity; an infinite island of self, in the boundless ocean of Self.

This is alchemical individuation- the creation of the indestructible diamond body, the ascension into the eternal realm, the apotheosis of the profane self, the addition of a permanent spice into the great stew of being, distinct but not separate, an inimitable lotus blooming above the illimitable mire.

Thus only the inner maverick makes it across into nothingness with yet his small self still in tact. Only the maverick transports eternity into now, infinity into the infinite, the ocean into the drop. Because the maverick has broken free from the paradigm, and yet remains within the paradigm in order to transform it. This is the renegade within who is Christ.

Only such ones, who are not of the paradigm, but are of themselves, can be in the paradigm unscathed. Belief in oneself is the only validation of one's eternity. To know *and* to be. In *and* of.

The microcosm is the actualized, manifest tension between macrocosmic energies. To exist as a microcosmic eternity is to be a living nexus between dynamic forces, and therefore to ever be pushed and pulled within by invisible struggles. This is to be outside of duality and the battle between opposed energies, but therefore to be the battlefield itself.

*

five

Under the sky, and upon the earth, we continued our stay in Goa.

A couple of sublime cosmic happenings poked their heads out of the ether while we were there.

Firstly, and interestingly enough, given the events of which I have just spoken, while staying in that pristine beach village, my *soror* and I had serendipitously been guided to rent a room from an emanation of the Mother[31].

I conclude that no matter how far I tried to flee from Her after Calcutta, She was ever present in my life.

And secondly, I suddenly recalled the original dream I had of the Dingle Peninsula in Ireland, which had sent us to that sacred area now half-way around the world. In the dream of Dingle there had been many houses build on stilts, but in actuality there are no such houses like these in Dingle. However, there are many such huts like these in Goa.

As well, from the middle of the beach town that we were staying at in Goa, the view south looked incredibly similar to the Kerry peninsula, which runs south of the Dingle. The similarity was striking. And not only that, there were two small islands off of Goa, as one looked southward down the coast, which appeared quite like Skelig Michael and Little Skelig- the monastic islands off the coast of Kerry- and the Goan islands were visually in the exact same relative position as those off of Kerry. This was indeed an odd coincidence in a world where there is no such thing as coincidence. Oh no, this realm is subtly choreographed and administered by the great architects beyond all knowing. All places and people are sacred and surreal. All events are holographic and holy. Nothing happens separately from the rest. Everything is intermingled, mirrored, and interwoven in a divine matrix of psychedelic obscurity and wonder. Even Goa.[32]

---

[31] This woman was from a different archetypical pattern than the Mother emanation who sent us off from the Vancouver airport at the beginning of our trip. But to be sure she was a true aspect of the Goddess. I recognized her instantly because she could have been the younger sister of a good friend of ours who is an embodiment of the Mother. This archetype must exist quite frequently in manifestation at this time, because we ran into another emanation of Her earlier in Amritsar, and at the time of writing this I am working closely with another woman who is almost identical to these other three, though none of them know of each other and to the best of my knowledge live in different corners of the globe. But that's the necessity of the oversoul's emanations, which exist within different geographical dramas so as to branch out and experience the world in multifarious ways.

[32] In fact, during our stay in Goa, I recognized an incredible assortment of differing archetypes who in the past I had known in different bodies, as different 'types'. No doubt this is a function of the very nature of my own soul which, like everyone else's, draws to it the differing spices and ingredients which make up its cosmic stew. Most of the 'types' I recognized were of archetypes that are very close to the core of my being. I suppose this explains why in esoteric tongue it is said that every individual is a universe unto themselves. If this is the case, then the archetypes which have been swirling about my being ever since birth are similar to the planets which orbit a sun.

I say 'even' Goa because many people consider Goa to be a mecca for hedonism, licentiousness, and distraction, and therefore devoid of any religious or spiritual significance whatsoever. And, to be sure, all of the aforementioned profane practices exist in great quantity in that small Indian state that is perhaps visited by more westerners than the rest of India combined.

However, I consider Goa holy. As holy as anywhere else. For how could a place brimming with thick forests, rolling green hills, endless magnificent beaches, friendly people, marvelous sunsets, and wholesome food be other than holy? In my mind Goa is a temple of the earth, not to mention a unique commingling of Christian practices hybridized with Indian devotion.

But, as I said, most people view it as otherwise.

A Latin fellow I met during our time there had been living in India for the past seven years, and had wandered as a barefoot pilgrim from holy site to holy site, living along the Ganges for much of his stay, and moving in the presence of a spiritual master for some of that time. This Latin man, who had renounced his earlier life for the higher calling, spoke with great contempt for Goa, claiming that it was an unholy place full of stupid people.

Unfortunately for him, as I know only too well, his 'spiritual' life and rarified contemplations had placed him outside of the flesh and the earth, and had prevented him from recognizing his own body as an inner sanctuary within this great temple of the earth called Goa. From his rarified vantage point he could *see* only the stupid and superfluous human activities, instead of *feeling* the glory of the sacred earth.

For in Goa the true *sadhu* does not come with begging bowl in hand, mantra on his lips, nor scorn for worldly ways on his mind. No, the true earth *sadhu* arrives in Goa with an awe and rapture for the beauty of this spectacle of matter. The true Goan *sadhu* lies beneath the warm and limitless sun, walks upon the endless, unforgettable shore, and bathes not at the holy ghats of

---

I maintain, once again, that this is an incredibly difficult and hidden pattern of the spirit to explain. The only way to recognize the archetypes/oversouls, is to witness how the inner spirits of some people who come into your life are almost identical to others whom you have met. These are the types/souls which belong to the same fundamental branches- the archetypes/oversouls- on the Tree of Life.

the Ganges, but in the tropical, saline blood of the welcoming Indian Ocean.

The true, flesh and blood Goan *sadhu* fills his belly not with austere alms, but with a generous plate of sumptuous kingfish, washed down with a tall, cold, and bubbly Goan beer. Then he walks out into the star-riddled night, before wandering back to his hut and making love to his mate.

For it is in Goa that a person does not find God in the lofty reaches of the empyrean spirit, but instead in the dark and delicious, divine incarnation of the flesh.

This Latin fellow is an interesting example of one who has yet to build the bridge between spirit and flesh. Although in his earlier days he had lived a sensual life, had been a successful musician, and a father, he eventually turned away from it all in the pursuit of his higher calling. However, there was still a great deal of wild sensuality within him, which he repressed to his own detriment. For if he had accepted this essential Dionysian aspect of his being, as well as his eastern mysticism, he would have spanned the gap that divides Heaven and Earth, and would have become an amalgamation of St. Francis of Assisi, and Casanova. A rare, wholly combination indeed.

Nevertheless, he and I, being two imperfect blokes, enjoyed each other's company during our brief time together.

After all, I had now fully accepted my substance, and so had unified the subtle, eternal consciousness, with gross, immortal matter. And when that is done in a place like Goa, there is nothing left to do but do nothing.

To remain in a place like Goa, where no effort is required to maintain life's inherent needs, is to arrive in the realm of effortlessness. And since every day is like every other day, time slows down and eventually disappears altogether, as each new day blends seamlessly in with the last, and only the eternal, flowing now remains.

When such a timeless state occurs, and all unnecessary variables of life are removed, the effortless self cannot help but rise like a distillate out of the ore.

I had experienced similar effortless timeless periods in the past while camping for lengthy durations in the wilderness, or while caretaking remote coastal cabins and lodges. But now I was in Goa, living softly amidst the soft breeze and infinite ocean. And so I became like the soft breeze and the infinite ocean. Which is to say, I knew once again that it is a beautiful thing... to *be*. I had arrived.

To become effortless is to be the eternal, effortless self. And I was becoming more and more effortless. I was blending gently into Her.

At one point I became so consciously empty and effortless, that a cow which had been grazing nearby must have picked up on my similarly docile vibration, and turned slowly towards me with a curious look, and then meandered over as if to say "Welcome to the ambitionless club."

This may sound like a bit of useless fable or unnecessary trivia, but the soul within recognizes the subtle yet profound shifts which transform who we once were into another being altogether. The external world may have no clue that a new person now stands before them, but the soul knows, and that is all that matters. And at the moment I- an effortful, accomplishing male-recognized effortlessness, and become effortless, an immense shift happened- I became en*light*ened. Which is to say, I lay down and an immense amount of energy poured in and through me; the cellular structure of my being transformed; the matter of my body entered a higher vibrational rate, as it was infused with the cosmic light from above.

I became lighter of mind, and lighter of body. My en*light*enment had nothing to do with knowledge or realization, but in 'lightening' up, both figuratively and actually.

At the critical union of spirit and flesh, in the effortless awareness of my subtle, eternal being, my gross body was elevated energetically, and it became new. I was transfigured.

That is when I understood Christ's statement- "If thine eye be single thy whole body will be full of light."[33] This is the true en*light*enment, which has nothing to do with wisdom, but is instead the raising of matter to the vibration of light.

When mind and matter are one, and the mind 'lightens up', the body must go with it.[34] This is the elevation of the Mother and all of matter into the higher vibrational rate of spirit.

---

[33] ie: the third-eye, in which union of the opposites takes place. When the two halves of God unite within you and take up conscious residence behind the third-eye, that is when you have entered the inner sanctum. That is when you can be totally, inviolably inside yourself *and* totally, sensitively, intimate with others and the world.
[34] I once had a dream in which my *anima* (my inner female self) was trying to show me how to fly. As soon as she began to float away, off of the ground, she started yelling back to me- "Everything is light! Everything is light!", and I knew that her lightness of being was

To go down into matter, the Mother, to love Her, and to rise with Her into the Father's light, is to become the earth ascending.

When the vibration of spirit unites with the vibration of flesh, a whole new harmony is created; a oneness containing all dualities: male and female, consciousness and matter, good and evil, self and other, macrocosm and microcosm, inside and out.

Through my male side I had received Krishna's limitless, liberated consciousness; through my female side I attained union with all matter, the Mother, the entire manifested, warm and integral cosmos. I united spirit and flesh, consciousness and form, and male and female within and as me. I became one with all.

I did not simply come to earth, I *became* the earth, for I found that finite, manifest existence does not confine the infinite, eternal Self; it completes it. For these two in union become a whole new third event- one great, unified, manifest emptiness.

As humanity evolves, this essential unity will bridge all divisions and dissolve all separations. This wholeness will create an all-pervasive consciousness/being, where every I is part of every other I. All of life will then be linked in a divine matrix of spirit and flesh. All individuals will then become unique patterns on the same cosmic carpet; all souls will be distinct, but not separate. One. *Om, baby!*

*

six

When seen from the immense, untroubled distance of the cosmic eye, everything on earth seems placid, well-balanced, fluid, and as it should be. It's like when we look upon a city at night from a distant hill and see only beautiful lights twinkling serenely off in the distance. From such a remote outlook none of the noise nor pandemonium, none of the violence nor anguish, none of the sex nor seduction, nor the dance, the merriment, the corruption, congestion, nor confusion is betrayed for the actuality that it is. From such a distance one may quickly draw the

---

directly related to 'lightening up', as they say. This is the en*light*enment which is of the flesh, not of the mind.

conclusion that nothing really happens there but a gentle and calm twinkling of pretty lights.

It is the same when we look up into the glorious night sky. Above us we see only a breathtaking display of brilliant stars consuming an immensity that is well beyond our ability to comprehend. We can see nothing of the warfare, the plunder, the thrashing, the sorrow, the rage, nor the ecstasy, the love, nor the celebration. From our distance even the apocalyptic violence of a supernova appears as a gorgeous spectacle. We do not hear nor feel the agony of the billions of souls incinerated in the inferno.

Our distance has created an 'object' *from* which we are detached, and with which we are therefore no longer intimate.

It is for this reason that in this era of new age ideas and spiritual charlatans, there are many individuals who claim that all of life is illusion- that existence as we know it is nothing but a dream of the mind. And I now realize this to be an understandable conclusion for anyone who has awoken to transcendental consciousness, but who has yet to awaken to the immanent soul of matter. For when transcendental consciousness happens, and one is suddenly 'outside' of all that is, and one can thus see from a detached perspective that all is but a divine drama which is acted out by sleeping actors, it is quite understandable that one would fall away with a great sigh of relief, having found a safe distance from the turmoil of existence, and remain there, comfortable in the knowledge that all of life is an illusion, and that they are now thankfully free from that illusion. However, I now know this to be a disastrous conclusion.

For whether it be a distant cosmic happening, or a nearby earthly event, none of it matters a scratch to consciousness until the spirit descends into the awaiting maelstrom, and learns for itself the truth and actuality of what it means to truly *be*. This is the Christ born into matter.

It is true that human existence, when looked at from afar, appears to be of the nature of a divine drama, a play, a *lila*, as it is called in India, which runs on eternally. But it is only from such a remote perspective of the cosmic eye that life on earth may then be called an illusion. A more appropriate term for the nature of such a perspective would be 'misperception', in that such a distant consciousness 'misperceives' the true nature of what it means to be human.

To conclude, therefore, that all matter is unreal simply because the human drama is dreamlike is like assuming that simply because a television show is fictitious, the television is unreal as well.

The difficulty for the mind comes in recognizing that the world is real not at the level of the human drama, but at the level of the soul; and therefore to attain transcendental consciousness is to be liberated from the profane paradigm, from *maya*, but not from the divinity of matter itself.

True liberation is to be 'liberated' from the drama, but not from existence itself, for existence is the essence of the soul, and consciousness is the essence of the spirit, and peace is the essence of their union.

In the attainment of one's wholeness and true nature, the projected outpouring of one's existence transforms out of a drama and into a documentary; for now all of one's actions within the paradigm are *actual* and true expressions of the eternal self, rather than mere entertainments looked upon from a detached creator.

In this sense we descend from the metaphor into the actual, and from the projection onto the scene. The only illusion is illusion. Alchemical individuation is the moment when we become *real*, and not merely phantom actors in the show, for we must come to earth completely, if we are ever to be completed.

To emanate as the sun emanates is to have no relationship to that which has a relationship to you, for the sun would exist without us, but not we without the sun. This is the great transcendence from this plane. However, it is only when the sun and moon- the male and female- are in union, and the sun is energetically drawn into creation, that creation becomes one with the sun.

The sun must love the moon for such a cosmic marriage to bring redemption to the dark world. And so we only truly rise up in our perfection by first descending as God onto Earth, and then rising as the Earth up with God.[35]

---

[35] It is foretold that the next incarnation of Vishnu- following Krishna and the Buddha- will be Kalki, the one who will complete the work that both Krishna and Buddha began, thus bringing the divine firmly down to earth, to Avalon. It is said that he/she will be the one to bring ..."the kingdom of the Divine upon Earth." (Sri Aurobindo, *Sri Krishna*, p30. SABCL, Vol. 22), and "...the last Avatar, Kalki, only accomplishes the work Krishna began..." (Sri Aurobindo, *Essays on the Gita*, p157). If this is an odd bit of news to swallow, let us remember that the Buddha himself touched the earth as a witness to his enlightenment, and therefore validated matter as a true actuality.

As I have said, to stand apart from being, emancipated into transcendental consciousness, is an immensely important function for humanity to become capable of, though no more important than our descent into the very core and absoluteness of this earthly paradigm of flesh.

In the end we must expand in both directions if we are to have the wisdom of a cosmic spirit, and the heart of an earthly soul. We must unite revelation with actualization, *jnana* with *bhakti*[36], and so catalyze the transfiguration arising from the union of spirit and flesh.

I accept that I am a part of this process- the process of merging the spirit into the earth- as most of us likely are. I have in the past had many dreams in which my body and the bodies of a few other individuals were covered completely in a layer of green leaves. I had no idea what this symbol indicated until I came upon information about The Green Man, a mythological character who arrives to resuscitate mankind's intimacy with the earth. In mythological pictures he is shown covered in leaves.

I can therefore declare with awe and humility that we are not here to abandon the mystic flesh, but to exalt it. We are not here to be liberated *from* this realm, but to be liberated *within* this realm.

To bring infinity into the finite is to transform the great cosmic stillness into the great cosmic dance; it is to combine into oneself the dual energies of Vishnu and Lakshmi, Radha and Krishna, Shiva and Shakti, Jesus and Mary, and to merge these within oneself, all the while flowing in, and of, and through the light and dark turmoil of this mad, marvelous mystery.

To mix the infinite into the finite is to blend the finite into the infinite until they are interwoven and indistinguishable.

To be the emptiness that is a living bridge between the Mother and Father is to mix consciousness and matter into one indistinguishable, viscous fluidity, and so to merge into and become an ocean of beingness, lighter than matter, and denser than mind.

The archetypical and eternal forces then awaken in the drama. The invisible Self animating the visible self becomes everything. The macrocosm becomes the microcosm, the word is

---

[36] *jnana* is the Sanskrit word for wisdom, or knowledge; *bhakti* is the Sanskrit word for devotion. Thus one represents the mind, the other the heart.

made flesh, and all that is mundane becomes transmogrified into the song of the Divine. *Om, baby!*

*

Part IV
MYSTERIUM CONIUNCTIONIS

"In the grand cosmological dance of the universe, nothing is ever lost, only transfigured."
Leigh McCloskey[37]

---

[37] *Tarot Revisioned.* Olandar Press, US. 2003

one

For one to arrive at the empty core from which all existence radiates, the alchemical union of a number of opposites existing within the individual is required. Without such unions there can be no circle, and therefore no hollow core.

Alchemy is the process by which a mortal becomes immortal, and is a very specific journey for each individual.

The goal of alchemy is individuation- the immortalization of the soul. To individuate, which is to become whole, requires the union of male and female, good and evil, spirit and soul, consciousness and matter, subject and object, self and other, and inside and out.[38]

To become immortal is to turn the gross lead of mortality into the subtle gold of eternity.

To unify the male and female within requires a man to become conscious of his inner female, his *anima*, and a woman to become conscious of her inner male, her *animus*[39].

Such integration takes determination, patience, and the willingness to transform. The outcome of this union within the individual is the *sacred androgyne*, which is the divine, incarnate soul, awake as an androgynous self within the androgynous universe. This comes about through the inner *chymical wedding*, which represents one of the final stages of alchemy.

---

[38] As in the Gospel of Thomas (#22), where Jesus stated that one would enter the kingdom of spirit: "When you make the two one, and when you make the inside as the outside, and the outside as the inside, and the upper side as the lower; and when you make the male and the female into a single one, that the male be not male and the female not female…"

[39] *anima* is the Latin word for 'soul, *animus* is the Latin word for 'spirit'.

This is a picture of my *soror*. I have added a line to make it easier to recognize the physiological bifurcation of her face, where one half is male, and the other half female, and one eye is smaller and farther forward than the other. The dual nature of the face is a common occurrence in individuals who have at lease partly assimilated their inner, alter-gender self.

In Hindu mythology this holy completion is represented by the God Ardhanarisvara, who is the union of Shiva and Shakti. Ardhanarisvara's right side is male, and his/her left side is female.[40]

---

[40] Many times pieces of writing would come to me in order that they might emphasize and/or support a realization I had recently perceived. As such, soon after my own experience of the union of transcendental consciousness and immanent being creating the androgynous nature of existence- and at that time feeling my left side to be female, and my right to be male- I came across this passage: "We cherish in our hearts this pure ethereal Consciousness, which, in conjunction with its free Sakti (supreme power), emanates as the Supreme Truth...and which is in a constant state of joyous dance, that enables all to realize the wonder of the experience of Nondual Bliss. May we have the protection of that form, the left side of which is the Mother of the entire universe that exists, the right side of which is the Father of the entire universe that exists..." *Ribhu Gita* 1:2 (Trans. by Dr. H. Ramamoorthy and Nome. Society of Abidance in Truth, California. 2003)

Ardhanarisvara

Ardhanarisvara is the symbol of cosmic androgyny.

This subtle, archetypical, androgynous blue-print filters down and infiltrates all aspects of the universe. Therefore, just as Krishna and his consort Radha became inseparable aspects of their common being, many thousands of years ago, to such an extent that in later Hindu writings these two were called by a singular name- RadhaKrishna- so too we must all become both the male-outside-of-existence, cosmic consciousness- and the female-inside-of-existence, earthly being.

This union takes place at the third-eye chakra, which is the epicenter and vessel into which the male descends from non-being, and the female rises from being.

Until union occurs at third-eye via the kundalini, duality is unavoidable. After meeting at the third-eye, the opposite aspects of existence begin to unite and the individual attains the recognition of universal oneness.

When this integration begins to take place, a subtle, ethereal wind may be felt flowing onto the third-eye. This is the beginning of a different type of breathing- it is the breath of consciousness itself, the breath of ascension.

Transcendental consciousness and immanent being have thus begun to come together as integrated emptiness/being.

To be the whole Self is to be the intimate union of non-being and being, of male and female, of the immense, still, empty consciousness, *and* the active, dynamic, ubiquitous form.

One intimate union. One.

*

two

The next essential unification to occur within the individual is that of good and evil. In order to merge good and evil one must acknowledge their own depravities. This is a difficult inner accomplishment, because most of us inherently think we are good, and believe that only other people are bad. However, this universe is a mixture of the two, and anyone who believes they are good only will no doubt have the truth brought before them in unavoidable fashion, for goodness does not exist without badness.[41]

I have been, in the past, a great hypocrite of this inexorable duality of good and evil, thinking that I was a 'good' person, and therefore repressing the truth of my darkness. The acknowledgement that I was a criminal took many years to come to consciousness, as I was forever believing myself to be full of light and beyond evil.

In the end, however, I had to admit the truth, which is a painful but necessary acknowledgement for anyone who seeks to expand into the greater reality beyond the drama of duality.

---

[41] It is for this reason that Christ himself admonished his disciple for thinking Christ was something that he wasn't; after his disciple had stated how 'good' Christ was, Christ categorically retorted: "Do not call me good."

These acknowledgements that I made are the spiritual scars of growth which dwell in the heart of every sinner. And if that sounds like a confession, perhaps that is what it is. I look back on my life now with intent only to see myself for what I am, or have been. And what I have been, at times, is a wild child, a deceiver and a thief. In short, a criminal who had broken the one and only law, which is love.

In fact, God the Father had to come to me one time and state with harsh directness: "Seek your own upliftment, not another's downfall". This because I had fallen into darkness, and was not focused on the most perfect expression of my highest path, being at that time tangled in judgment and thoughts of less than love towards others.

I look back now with both a shudder and a smile, as I recall the ways in which I betrayed myself and others. Oh, in the unrelenting, perilous throes of sin, like a thief too afraid to steal, I was given everything I needed, though inside myself I still plotted and squirmed.

Yea, like a bivalve of the spirit- relentless miracles through me went, though I remained separate and intolerable. I was a horrid creature of grace.

I was Abraham, recklessly pursuing Isaac- escaped, terrified and weeping- down the precipitous slopes of my own tortured delusion. There was no economy in my strides. There was no promise within me, not a single resolution. Why the crowds of passing daemons did not spit on me in disgust, I shall never know; a sinner amongst saints, dog-shit on a manicured lawn, a booger on a bare wall, a cyst on supple flesh. At times every breath I took left another scar upon the earth. What ghastly errors I spawned onto life.

While my penance flamed into its full and ruthless glory, how deep indeed I was buried in ignorance, and darkness.

All this happens so secretly- intoxication with the Worm, I mean- but, man alive, it happens. Let me tell you, I did not rise piously out of the noxious mist, but instead inhaled its toxic qualities, in the spineless hyperventilation of agreeable illusions. Oh, I had breathed in heavily for such a time- those musty, hallucinogenic vapors of my own criminal expulsion- that I lived in a vacuum, in the nauseous stench of my own halitotic excuses and demands.

Like a runaway angel kidnapping the light, feeding the darkness with my own estrangement, and souring the love with my flight, I was afoul. Like the wretched concubine of a syphilitic Love, I was royalty in the morning, a servant by noon, and a lost thief fleeing by night. I stole from life's treasures, and poached sacred trophies from the kingdom's sparse herd.

And though the magic was boundlessly making me, all I did was get in the way. Many benedictions I swallowed, but often only calumnies were expelled. And the same hands, thanklessly receiving the manna of heaven, returned it but shortly, as vomit.

Further, and further, down and down came the inescapable fall. What was life to me, after all, but a looting? I was consumed by both the heights and the depths, by the unknown and the known, while I hovered in between at a spot where I was equally destroyed by both; I had reached an equilibrium that was not peace, an inaction that was not serenity.

As if the angel had tripped while carrying me, and I was fumbled into unrecognizable positions, tumbling about in her frantic hands, with her struggling to keep me off the moribund ground; I was not dropped, though neither was I caught gently in the air.

There was no such noble act of willful becoming for me, only a coasting down the hill without an engine, enjoying the ride to hell. I was a thief, a criminal. I had fallen from the golden rule of love. I was separate.

Oh there was a time, as the Fates merged upon the barren battleground that I called me, when I could neither fully believe nor fully disbelieve existence. I had lost both truth and untruth, having no foothold in myself, nor in the world; neither in the mundane, nor the spiritual.

These were the trials of my idiosyncratic becoming, of God and Satan making folly in my breast.

Oh, I stumbled, I crashed, through rack and ruin, beating blindly without reason, seeking to find some sort of serenity, or to die within feet of the door.

I was in prison and did not know it, for I had cast less than love upon my brothers and sisters in this world, and when one does that, one goes to hell.

Oh Lord, oh Lord, I am also why the world is the way it is. I have spread much sorrow upon this earth. I have sown grief without intent to harvest. I have carried the seeds of my discontent and scattered them into the lives of others. I have spent my days abandoning love, irrigating my parched life with other's tears. Oh, the scars I have irreverently furrowed upon this globe.

Lord, I was a confused and reckless farm-hand. I am sorry for the hate, the lies, and the worry. Forgive my ingratitude. Guide me to love, and let me not wander. Forgive me for having planted misery into the fallow hearts of others.

These were the beseeched cries I lamented into the cosmos as I came upon the criminal within me. It was horrible. But it was necessary. For if I was to merge with the all, I had to become harmonious with the all, which was to be conscious I was both good and evil, and so neither.

The absolute merging of these polarities began after I had a strong astral dream in which I encountered- as in the past- the deep, dark, aggressive and terrible force of Satan. And, as in the past, I was saved by calling on Christ. This time, however, the encounter was different from the others, for this time Satan was not outside of me, he was *inside*.

After waking from that astral encounter I immediately began intentionally directing my consciousness towards Christ and his protection of me. I wanted to distance myself as far as possible from Satan. But then it occurred to me that what was necessary now was not further division, but union- union of the opposites of good and evil.

I then began merging Satan and Christ within me- the absolute, loving, good light, *and* the absolute, oppressive, evil darkness. Instantly I inwardly saw a black and white checkered pattern emerge, and I felt peace.[42]

Moments later I had a vision of an old alchemist holding an orb made of precious metals inlaid with gems and he was offering it to me: a symbol of the whole self.

---

[42] Interestingly enough, in alchemical literature, Christ's older brother is called Satanael.

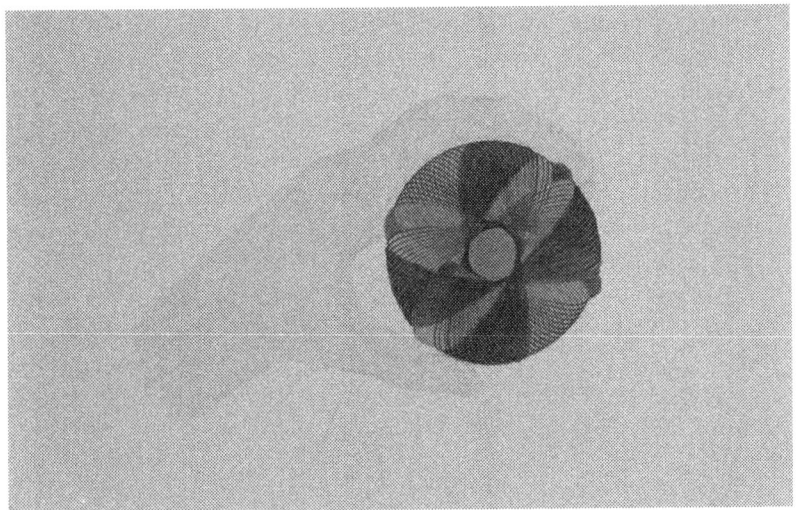

A rough likeness to the orb given to me by the alchemist.

The following morning my *soror* informed me that Carl Jung stated that a person needed to merge their male and female sides before he or she could merge their light/good and dark/evil halves. I had done so without prior knowledge of this process, though with a great amount of guidance from higher spirits.

And so I say that if you would take Satan within yourself, you better also have Christ in there, or you'll be in for some big trouble, as it is only the balancing power of the light which makes integrating the darkness possible.[43]

---

[43] As an aside I must note that in contemporary alchemical and psychoanalytical understanding, Satan- also known as the 'demon lover', or Devil- is considered to be the repressed female *animus*, and since women have been repressed for centuries, that force is very strong, and very angry. Given this information, the 'devil' that I encountered could have been my *soror's* repressed animus. However, all things being one event, the truth of this 'evil' is somewhat more complicated than one of simple gender domination. This is because both individuals within an intimate relationship are each only one half of the whole. Therefore the Devil, hidden in a woman's psyche, often becomes manifest in her male partner, which is why most atrocities and evil acts are committed by men. Furthermore, much of the 'evilness' in the man comes from repressing his *anima*- his inner female- which manifests in his female partner- the repressed female whose repressed *animus* is the Devil. This is a cyclic and reciprocal relationship, and therefore the man and the woman in the union are equally responsible for the repression and/or growth of the other, for they are one.

This claustrophobic, unconscious nightmare is healed only as the man takes on his female side, and the woman her male side; the repression and concomitant 'evil' will begin to decline, and, after assimilating the repressed and, so to speak, 'Devilish' aspects of each person, wholeness will blossom for both, who are one.

To become whole, which is to become one with the whole, means to exclude nothing. In this case one must recognize that they are both good and bad, which means being Satan as well as Christ. It is best therefore, as I have said, to become Christ first, for only then can the dark be assimilated without destroying you. You must become Christ so that you can be Satan Christed. Good and Evil. One. No longer either good or evil, but instead a whole new awoken, eternal Zen neutrality.[44]

When looked upon closely the characteristics of the divine are ever intermingled with good and evil. And that is because at the level of divinity, where good and evil merge into one, there is no longer good or evil, there is simply a dynamic dance beyond the limited idea of morality.[45]

---

[44] I find it necessary to draw a distinction here between one's own, inner darkness, which must be united with the dark aspect of the universe, and the evil spirits and demons that lurk in the spirit realm, which must be repelled and destroyed. The former aspect of evil is metaphysical, the latter is shamanic; to own one's inner darkness is essential in coming to wholeness, however, there is no need to then believe that one is beyond fighting against evil in the world. Although I have admitted my own darkness, I still adhere to the law of love, and to self preservation. With the help of Christ I have set myself against a number of demons intent on harming either myself or one I loved. It is important to recognize that there are indeed truly evil spirits which can invisibly enter a person's soul and do incredible harm, and therefore these must be met with as much force and fury as is necessary in order to drive them away. In this sense it is important to own one's own darkness and rage, for then this force can be a valuable weapon against such intruders. Therefore, to unite the light and the dark within yourself does not take you out of the arena of spiritual warfare, it merely makes you a more complete being.

[45] I am thinking here of the descriptions of two Tibetan Buddhist masters, Marpa and Milarepa, given by Fosco Maraini, an Italian researcher and explorer who penetrated into the protected borders of mysterious Tibet early in the twentieth century. His accounts of the country, its art, and its people betray the true light and dark quality of this 'holy civilization', a country which to the outside eye had given itself to the higher pursuits and had left the profane behind. However, every human atrocity imaginable was also present in that sacred land, as much as any other, for if truth be known, to seek the light is to be confronted by the shadow.

Maraini's description of the Tibetan Buddhist master Marpa runs: "...a doctor learned in esoteric knowledge, a pugilist, a violent, quarrelsome, proud, temperamental man, eternally dissatisfied because of the unattainability of perfection, given at times to drunkenness, unfairness or cruelty, a kind of natural genius with the spirit of lightning and the splendour of a storm." And Maraini's equally nonpartisan description of Milarepa states that this Buddhist master was a "...wizard, hermit, poet, philosopher, sinner, a tumultuous soul ever in anguish or frenzy, with an unlimited capacity for both good and evil, and unbounded spiritual energy..."[45] In fact Milarepa had been a murderer earlier in his life, and yet he had attained complete emancipation from the round of birth and rebirth. Of course, he had to go about it in the opposite way from most of us; Milarepa had to accept and assimilate his goodness, his 'light' side. Most of us must instead wrestle with our darkness.

These two liberated souls are not unique cases hauled out of an improbable cultural milieu so as to validate my thesis. We must recall that St. Paul was originally Saul, a brutal oppressor and tyrant, and yet Christ chose him, over of all others, including Christ's

If all is one, then good and evil must coexist, not as separate halves of the dual universe, but as intimate aspects of the One.

If God is everything there is, then there is no right or wrong, for all is one and no duality about it. Good and Evil end not because they do not exist, but because they become the same thing.[46]

Just as a battery requires both negative and positive poles in order to produce electricity, which is power, so to the negative and positive- the dark and the light- must exist within the individual and the universe for the proper functioning of the whole. Yin and yang.

However, the concept of good and bad only applies to the world of duality, it does not apply to the non-dual oneness which exists prior to the divisive 'fall' into manifestation.

It is only after the merging occurs of these opposites and a neutral wholeness arises, creating a further dimension of cosmic vision, that one can come to know the true nature of the human drama, which is indeed a drama- an eternal play enacted by eternal characters who somehow have forgotten they are acting.

It is the combined distance and intimacy of this new wholeness which allows the theater of all life to lay itself down before you, showing indisputably that the relative plane of human interaction is but a play, created by, and for, the Godselves which we are. This is the *lila*- the Divine Play- of life, and is the reason that the great incarnate, Krishna, could on one occasion send Arjuna to the battlefield to slay his own kin, and could at another time disrobe the young female cowherds and enjoy the pleasures of the flesh with them, without there being a contradiction in his actions.

Krishna had stepped outside of karma, outside of separation, outside of good and evil, outside of what we mistakenly call reality, and he lived knowing that all is a play, and

---

most intimate disciples. And then there was Mohammed, a warrior as ruthless and compassionless as they come, and yet he was Allah's chosen leader. And how about the Norse God Thor, remembered most often for his war hammer? And what of the Greek pantheon replete with Gods and half-gods ever consumed with conflict and atrocities?
[46] "You may be not aware that the English word 'devil' comes from the same root as the word 'divine'. Both come from the Sanskrit root: the Sanskrit root is *dev*. *Dev* means god, divine, devata. From *dev* comes the English word 'divine', and from *dev* comes the English word 'devil'. Both are divine. Both are one." Osho (*Vedanta: the supreme knowledge*, p100. Diamond Pocket Books, New Delhi, 1997)

that this is why we should play, because all the struggle and strife, the tears and the anguish, are but perfectly choreographed performances to keep us from awakening to the show.

Krishna understood that no one ever dies, since he knew that we are all immortal, in one way or another, though most of us are asleep in the dream that is the play of our immortal self.

The entire play, like all plays, is based on attraction and repulsion between the opposites, which is why romance and conflict are great themes in both life and cinema. But when the opposites of male and female, and good and evil, dissolve into a singular homogenous milieu, the whole drama suddenly exposes itself because the play runs out of scenarios. The stream has run its course. All conflict has been resolved. The self has entered the serene abode, the Tao.

In fact, I once had a dream in which I was told the Devil was created in order to counterbalance God. This is so because good and evil are aspects of the same oneness, and therefore they are written into the play to give it some action.

In another of my dreams a few years back, the Father aspect of God dressed me up as a woman, and then in the dream I was forced to enter into a tremendous battle, but at the moment the two opposing armies came directly into vicious combat, the two sides suddenly transmuted into one, and the whole scene became a glorious, theatrical, operatic show. Good and evil, male and female had merged.

During another dream a cosmic dispensation was poured down upon me, in a way I had not expected, leading me into an awkward realization which had been trying to come into my consciousness for quite some time. It was an odd dream- I dreamt that a friend of mine named Chris was kissing the hairy belly of some unknown man. Then the dream shifted and I had suddenly received a haircut similar to those sported by the Hari Krishna's. I awoke and thought- what an odd and idiotic dream. However, as dreams are almost always symbolic, I began to uncover the hidden meaning of the dream.

Firstly, I already knew that whenever a person with the name 'Chris' appeared in one of my dreams, this was symbolic of an aspect of Christ. But why was Christ kissing the hairy belly of an unknown man? Admittedly I had no clue at first, although I assumed that he was symbolically pointing something out to me. And indeed, over the next while the understandings were slowly, though persistently, pushed upon me, as if the greater consciousness was saying- look here, since there's little chance you'll figure this one out, we'll give it to you straight, without all the symbolic mumbo jumbo.

And so I learned, through books on Hindu mythology, that 'Hari' is a popular name for Vishnu, and 'Hara' is a name for Shiva. Now, since 'Hari' is phonetically similar to 'hairy', and 'Hara' is a name for the midsection, or belly, of a person, it was obvious that this dream had nothing to do with a 'hairy belly', but instead a Hairy-Hara, or, Hari-Hara. I then learned that the name Hari-Hara is an infrequently used mythological term representing the amalgamation of Vishnu and Shiva, which is the union of the preserver and the destroyer, the light and the dark. An odd dream to be sure, but it was a significant herald telling me that Christ was symbolically pointing towards the great space beyond good and evil, which comes about from the union of these polarities.[47]

To mix the savior with the destroyer and become Hari-Hara, is to attain to the equilibrium of indifference.

In the past years of my growth I had experienced a great many 'hero' fantasies in which a violent atrocity was about to take place and I arrived to save the day. However, as my shadow came into consciousness I suddenly realized that the violent attacker was also myself.[48]

Yes, to admit to my own terribleness, to know myself a criminal, was to understand that I was both victimizer and hero, which is the end of both pride and shame. For to be both good and evil, cop and criminal, sage and scoundrel, Eli and Lucifer, Judas and Christ, light and shadow, is to depart from the psychological constraints of dualistic thinking, and to enter a wholly new vibration, a new realm. One.

This is to go beyond the duality of right and wrong, which is to enter the undivided unity of beingness. This is to stop eating of the fruit from the Tree of the Knowledge of Good and Evil- of correct and incorrect- and to begin again to eat from the Tree of Life, which is to return to the event at the moment of its God-

---

[47] "The ability to encompass the duality in life- suffering and joy, light and dark, growth and destruction, and to realize that they are one and the same, complementing each other like day and night. Hari-Hara is a living duality, symbolic of the reality that is manifest, through and contained within all living beings." Ganga Somany (*Shiva and Shakti*, p 24. Bookwise, New Delhi, 2002)

[48] A movie which dramatically shows the mergence of a man and his shadow is *The Fight Club*.

issuance, prior to the division of that One flow into two. For only the all can be One. To see this is to become a liberated neutral spirit. That is- to be able to see the dark and the light of every situation, removes the dark and the light, and leaves only the situation, which is the pristine, naked, ever-new now. *Om, baby!*

Yahoshuah-Maria[49]
A symbol of the union of male and female, light and dark.

*

---

[49] source unknown.

three

An important further integration for all of us, at this moment of our cosmic and earthly evolution, is the interpenetration of not only spirit and flesh, but also of *technology*. This may seem like an odd idea to insert into the running thesis of this work, but in fact there is a massive invisible clash of forces going on in the world, as these seemingly opposed aspects of universal oneness attempt to merge into this realm.[50]

I have had many experiences in which technology was symbolically intertwined with the spirit and flesh in order to help me unravel the confused course I did not know I was taking. Certain episodes of my inner life were reflected in 'technological' events around me. For example, on my second trip to India, eight years prior to my current journey, I carried with me an archaic laptop, and over the course of my stay, due to the rough and abusive conditions of numerous lengthy bus rides, the cells on the screen began to break apart and move around. At a point where approximately one-third of the cells had dislodged, their

---

[50] The movie *The Matrix* is an example of this theme. In the movie the lead character, Neo, is a master of the matrix, and in this way is a symbol of transcendental consciousness. However, Neo exists also in another realm- Zion. In my view, Zion represents the body (albeit the consciousness/matter event is somewhat turned upside-down by the movie, but nevertheless Neo is existing in two places at once- the dream world of the Matrix, and the real world of Zion). No doubt this is why the people of Zion had long, shaggy hair and dark skin, and enjoyed drums and dancing, for these are symbols of the earth and flesh. And, furthermore, the citizens of Zion *felt* love. And feeling belongs to the realm of the flesh and the soul.

Transcendental consciousness, when taken to the extreme, where everything is seen as illusion, expresses the essence of Neo's experience *in* the Matrix. However, such transcendentalism does not account for Neo's experience in Zion, which is the experience of the heart, of love, of the immanent soul. Hence Zion, again, is a place of long hair, drums, dancing, and soul-felt love, whereas the Matrix is a place of consciousness only- a mind-created reality.

Furthermore, in the movie there was a third aspect- the machine world. The movie was an attempt by its creator to assimilate not only the spirit and the flesh, but also technology- the machine world. However, the attempt symbolically failed. There was no assimilation, only a hiatus. At this point in the evolution of humanity I believe that the integration of these three aspects- spirit, flesh, and technology- is actually happening, and the author of the Matrix movie was subconsciously (or perhaps consciously) awakening to this integration.

It is now up to all of us to assimilate our own Zion with the machine world and the Matrix, creating a harmonious One. This is a tremendous, confused confluence however, and I, for one, do not know how long this integration will take.

movement had spread them all over the screen, and had formed a perfect image of the map of the world. Message: I am the world.[51]

Interestingly enough, at the end of that second trip, about four months later, those same cells had miraculously re-integrated themselves back into the screen, and the image had disappeared. The screen was once again almost as good as new. The image was gone, only the great space of oneness remained. The necessary message had been delivered, and then the slate had been wiped clean.

All is reflected through all. However, because of our singular vantage point within the infinite multiplicity of happenings, it is hard to perceive that we are the all in all, as much as anything else, all parts of which are only one thing. Rarely do we see the greater event, which we call the world, as a manifestation of our greater selves.

Another symbolic experience occurred, around the same time in my life, when I was planning to leave the remote southern area of the Queen Charlotte Islands, which are off the west coast of Canada- where I had been staying with a friend for over a month, during which time we had begun to quarrel and our brotherhood had turned sour, which caused me immense melancholy. The day before I was to leave I opened a book, which I had been carrying with me, on Dadaist art, and there, on the page I happened to turn to, was a painting by Giorgio de Chirico, titled *Melancholy of Departure*. The painting was comprised of a somewhat tangled factory or city scene (I was returning to the city), and an almost exact topographical sketch of the southern Queen Charlotte Islands. The likeness was inexplicable, and it was bewildering to see how perfect that spiritual mirror and symbology of my current life were presented to me.

---

[51] I am reminded here of Jiddu Krishnamurti's books, *You are the World*.

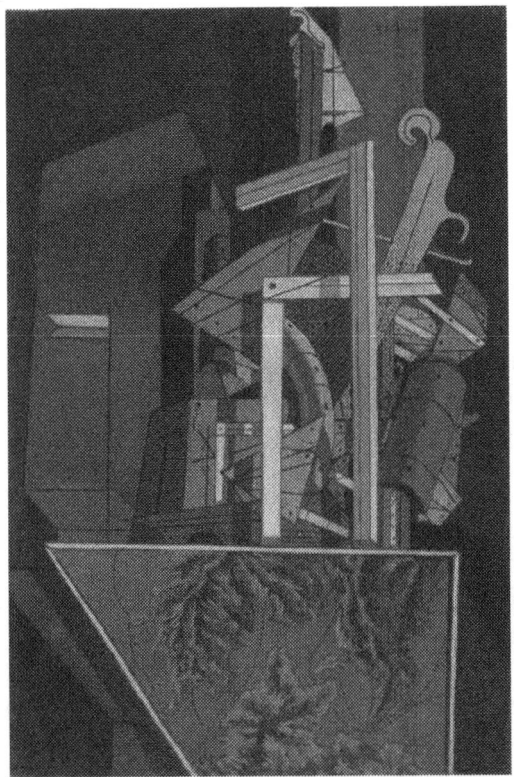

Melancholy of Departure by Giorgio de Chirico

Many times in my life such pieces of the puzzle would come flying out at me to make obvious my union with the whole, for all is reflected in all.

I wonder now if my entire life has been a project in which the macrosoul has been attempting to corral me into the places, experiences, and understandings which would help lead me to wholeness. Perhaps this is the reason why, as a youth, I would wake up almost every morning at exactly 7:37 a.m., like clockwork, as they say. Back then I found this extremely odd, and only later in life, as I was slowly accepting that the universe is a conscious universe, did I discover that the number 37 is the mystical number for the absolute union of spirit and soul. Wholeness.

Perhaps this macrocosmic intent is also why I had an experience, in my early thirties, while leaving Jerusalem, where I had gone for about a week while following the spirit of Christ. Not knowing what was to come next for me, I pronounced, as I was leaving, "Thy Will be done" with as much intent as ever I had before, and boarded the plane. Interestingly enough the in-flight entertainment on the plane was a British television show starring a younger version of my *anima* who was named Clarissa (clear Issa: Issa is the eastern name for Christ). This may seem like a wholly unprofound happening to the reader, but then it was *my anima* who was giving me the message, and the message was *clear*. For soon after that flight I was to become involved in a wild community within which were some very Christ-like women.

On another flight, this time off of the Big Island of Hawaii, which *is* the geophysical embodiment of the Mother, a man who was my father's spiritual archetype ended up sitting right behind me, which, if you know anything of such circumstances, is no mere coincidence, as if anything ever is. I was leaving the Mother and moving towards the Father.

Just prior to that flight I had been living on the Big Island of Hawaii and had no intentions of leaving. Then I had a dream in which I was shown a pair of green rain pants. I could not understand the dream until I felt compelled to leave Hawaii, the Mother, and flew back to Vancouver where I met with a good buddy of mine, who, at that time, was thoroughly united with the Father, and who was wearing the very pants I had dreamt about. Maddeningly enough this same buddy of mine was planning to visit me a month earlier in Hawaii, but backed out for various reasons. However, he and I were spiritual peers and our meeting was obviously necessary enough to have me called out of paradise and flown back to the rainy west-coast winter.

Then there was the time I dreamt of having my 7th tooth from the centre pulled out, and I had no idea what the dream meant. Not until a while later, when I picked up my harmonica and began playing it, and soon noticed that hole number 7 was no longer working. Something in me was 'out of tune' at that point.

This is similar to the time when I was learning to play the recorder, and I could not make any clear notes come out of the lower three of the seven holes. Not, at least, until I visited Hawaii for the first time, and, arriving on the Big Island, had the lower three of my seven main chakras stimulated and soon after could make perfect music come out of the lower notes of the recorder.[52]

---

[52] In esoterica, the seven main islands in the Hawaiian archipelago are said to represent the seven main chakras of the body. And, therefore, depending on what island you're visiting,

Not long after that I was given the present of a hand-made, Hawaiian bamboo-flute, which, oddly enough, and without the craftsman's intent, had the 7 holes of the flute laid out in a way astonishingly similar to the pattern of the Hawaiian islands themselves.

It seems to me that music must be an easy target for the muse of the spirit, since I can remember as far back as my early twenties, when I had purchased a copy of a *Midnight Oil* album which had on it the song *Bed's are Burning*, and that same night two futons were set ablaze accidentally in our apartment when my roommate's cigarette fell from his sleeping hand.

The internal is the external, and the external the in.

One of the ways this has become drastically obvious to me is through automobiles, for the vehicles in which people drive often reflect the nature of what is going on with them at the time.

For example, at a time when I was trying to find my voice in the world, I had a van in which the horn did not work.

I also know of a woman who, at a time in her life when she was very run down and often exhausted of energy, went through three alternators in less than a year.

Another woman friend, who developed a hard-to-diagnose yet chronic disease, had a vehicle which had an electric 'short' which mechanics were unable to find for almost five years. She was 'shorting out' within herself, and this was reflected in the manifest.

On a trip into the southwest American desert with my *soror*, a number of years back, we were heading into the Valley of the Gods, which is a remote, mythical landscape, carved out of the fleshy rock covering the area. We had intended to drive around a specific loop, and then find a campsite. As I say, we intended to do this, but the spirit had other ideas. Just as we were about to swing around that loop and leave a remote canyon area, one of the tires on our van blew out, and we had to pull over and repair it. A flat tire in the remote desert is an aggravating event, and I was aggravated. However, had we not been forced to stop in the exact spot where we stopped, we would not have later chosen a nearby campsite (instead of driving obliviously past it). And had we not camped in that exact spot, we would not have then been in the perfect perspective to see the gigantic sentinels and castle which

---

that chakra in your body will be stimulated. The Big Island represents the root, the lower chakra.

exist in the valley, the forms of which are a living reality on the subtle plane, and are manifest in stunning, megalithic rock sculpture on this material plane. We had been detained so that we would not miss out on the reason we had been guided there in the first place. As always, everything was as it should be.

In much less dramatic fashion, I learned a lesson about the intimacy of persons and vehicles at one point in my life when I was overly cognitive and contemplative, and had thoroughly abandoned the use of my feelings, instincts, and intuitions.

Fortunately I had purchased a small car in which the speedometer was not functioning. I say fortunately because although this was a very frustrating problem, as I never had any idea on how fast I was going, I soon learned to not need the conceptual boxes of thought and numbers, but instead to *feel* the speed at which I was going, which was a lesson in how not to *gauge* my life, but rather to live it.

I became so fluid with the vehicle that I rarely glanced at the dashboard- an event which I am always doing in vehicles whose speedometers are working- and yet never received a speeding ticket, for I inwardly knew from the *feel* of the vehicle the appropriate speed for the road.

I suppose this was an important lesson for me, because a while later I sold that car in northern Canada, spent some time in the wilderness, and then, before heading south, stayed at a friend's house for a week or two. It turned out that at that time he had another visitor, and since she was driving south at the time I needed to be heading that way myself, I took a lift with her and ended up behind the wheel for a greater part of the trip.

On the first day I was back to my old self, always looking at the speedometer- which on her car was working fine- for fear that I was driving too fast, or too slow. I was recognizing my pathetic dependence on the gauges, and thinking that I had not yet crystallized the lesson which was to 'feel' all of life, instead of 'think' it. But as night came on I was given some after-school tutoring, because when I went to turn the car lights on, I realized that the dashboard light in her car did not work, and so, at night I could not see the speedometer anymore. I was free of the mind again, and back into the feeling of body and flow of intimacy with being. For the mind is what divorces us from the fluid connection with life, and it is only feeling and intuition which rejoins us.

As a last point on the symbology of vehicles, I would note that often license plates betray a hidden anagram, or message, relevant to the owner of the vehicle at the time.

For example, a vehicle which my *soror* and I ended up owning together- at a time when we were starting to merge all opposites, including the light and the dark, and the east and the west- had a license plate which included the number 999, which is a mystical number unto itself, and is also 666 upside down.[53]

All things are alive and reflective of our inner beings, always.

I have heard that, prior to the sinking of the Titanic, there was a person who wrote a book about a grand cruise ship which sank in the north Atlantic on its first voyage, killing most of the people aboard. In the book the boat was called the *Titan*.

There are quite a few of these macrocosmic parallels to find, if you open yourself up to finding them.

All is reflected in all. All is all. It is only for us to learn a more holistic way of seeing.

At one point in my life I was in Ireland and asking for guidance as to whether I should stay where I was, or move on to Scotland. That night I had a dream in which I was drinking beer that was 5.9% in alcohol, and that was all I could remember upon waking. However, knowing that most Irish beers are around 4%, and that the Scots are intelligent enough to put a little more umph into their liquids, I jumped on a bus and headed north. Upon my arrival in Scotland I walked around curiously looking through liquor shops but could not find any beer that was exactly 5.9% alcohol. No matter. I had to leave the country a few days later, as I received word that a friend back home had been badly injured in an accident. So I returned to North America to see him, where, soon enough, I walked into a store, having forgotten all about my earlier dream, and stumbled right into a case of beer that was exactly 5.9% alcohol. I had come to where the spirit knew I would come, though I had had no clue about this at all.

God works within us with much greater intention than the hallmarked minutiae of life often betrays. But occasionally we get a glimpse of this incredible, hidden choreography running perfectly throughout the world, and that glimpse is sometimes enough to smash apart our limited conceptions, and expand us into

---

[53] I have recounted, at length, a very unique occurrence with license-plate messages in my book *Roots and Wings*.

union with the inexplicable all, which includes man-made creations and modern technology.

In fact, one time I dreamt that I was buying a Cadillac, and awoke without a single idea of what that would mean. Later that day, however, my *soror* was out and about on the town and was approached by a mad street-person who out of the blue, whimsically declared to her, "God is in town, and he's buying Cadillacs." *Om, baby!*

*

four

One of the last pair of opposites to unite into one is the duality of internal and external- that is, what we think of as inward, and what we experience as outward. To merge these two extremes is to feel the subtle unity of all things, and to collapse the subject and object duality. This is to see yourself as all others, and all others as yourself; it is to view yourself from an objective distance, just as you would view all external 'others', and to view all 'others' with a subjective intimacy, just the same as you would *feel* yourself within. This is to become no specific *I*, and therefore to be all *I's*.

Eventually my *soror* and I had to depart from the earthly glories of Goa and return to the worldly ways of Canada. However, before departing from India, we spent a few days in Delhi. This polluted, overcrowded, and chaotic metropolis might seem like the last place on earth that one would have a potent spiritual experience, but anything can happen anywhere in India where, after all, the gem is to be found in the shit.

By then I was becoming more and more immersed in the beings of the cosmic Goddess and God, so much so that while sitting cross-legged during the day in our tiny hotel room in Delhi I felt Shiva so completely that I *became* Shiva. Not the Shiva that is Nataraja- the dancing maniac bringing creative destruction to the world, but rather I became Shiva of the distant and contemplative Himalayas. Shiva the yogi. Shiva the silent one. Shiva the pristine, immoveable, limitless cosmic consciousness. I became enveloped in His spirit, and knew at that moment I *was* Shiva.

Then at night, in the depths of tranquility and peace, in the middle of the still darkness, I became enveloped in the thick, penetrating, fully ensconcing energy of Parvati's greater being, Devi, the One Goddess. Lying in bed, I merged into Her thick and fecund, glowing energy, and was united *in* Her.

This was a similar Mother-energy *samadhi* which I had experienced on the coast of British Columbia, on the Big Island of Hawaii, and in France, which are all places where such Mother energy is readily available. And now I had been received by Her in India.[54]

Anyone who has ever felt the immense, all-consuming energy of existence- the Mother- will in no way consider life as an illusion ever again, for they will know with an absolute, visceral, organic knowing that their being is actual, and is part of the living earth, and of all life.

This Mother energy *samadhi*- in which the individual is absorbed into and becomes the gyrating, ubiquitous, creative energy of the cosmos- which is to say, the individual attains union with God the Mother- is a rare experience in a world where most of us have been brought up not only in denial of the reality of our own flesh, but are also in denial of the livingness of the earth, and of matter itself. And it is not until we become our own flesh completely, and therefore unite with all matter- for all matter is one- that we can enter into the Mother's creative, all-ensconcing, primordial energy, and know for certain that the earth, the flesh, and all that is, is as real as real can be.

In the immense, intimate depths of the Goddess one realizes that the multiplicity and dynamic nature of form in no way modifies the infinity of Her eternity, because although form may change appearances, the essence of form- the Mother energy- is eternal.

These two unions and communions- with Shiva and Parvati, God and Goddess- are phenomena which cannot ever be fully explained, for they must be experienced. To become God the Father is to become Shiva, who is Isa, who is Issa, the eastern

---

[54] I read shortly afterward: "Those immersed in the ocean of Her substance, which is *citsakti* [Goddess consciousness], are forgetful of all differences which appertain to the world of form..." Sir John Woodroffe (*Hymns to the Goddess, and Hymn to Kali*, p vii. Ganesh and Company, Madras. 2001)

Christ. To unite with the Mother Goddess, Parvati, who is Devi, is to become the living cauldron of intense Goddess energy, which in the west has come to us as the Dark Madonna, an aspect of Mother Mary.

And from such experiences one comes to know that there are many names for the same Divine parents, but these are names only, and in the end there is no real division between eastern nor western spiritualities, but only diverse experiences arising from the one Godhead, which occur uniquely, depending on the cultural psyche and the disposition of the individual.

I find it no great surprise that my entire eastern journey began back in the west, in *The Baba* coffee shop in Amsterdam, a place dedicated to Ganesha- the initiator- the elephant-faced son of Shiva and Parvati.

I relate these experiences not from intent to isolate myself as someone more capable of spiritual accomplishments than another. The great souls themselves will bear witness to my torments and gnashings, my grievances and gross imperfections, my thievery and deceit. I am continuing to learn and grow. To make any claims about myself other than inherently possessing a relentless, unforgiving drive to accomplish my own emancipation, would be like attempting to bleach the dark earth Herself.

I have my darkness, my own desperations and limitations. But knowing this only too well gives me even greater incentive to write about my experiences, because I have encountered many obstacles along the way, and I am living proof ...that help is available. I have been given immense assistance and guidance, oftentimes beyond my ability to understand, to be thankful for, or perhaps even to recognize. But benevolence has watched over me. And knowing how my own journey has been so fraught with doubts and discontentment, I feel compelled to relate the profundity and importance of this help and guidance which is available to all who call out wildly in the confusing mist of the human night.

Indeed it may be a traumatic event to be born human. But I believe that the only person who will suffer in confusion and despair for lack of assistance is the one who does not ask for help.

I have asked many times. Oh, I have beseeched. I have prayed. I have pleaded. I have moaned for direction and succor. And I have also cursed and rebelled and stormed about in abject disgust. I have rambled and roamed unbridled at times like a madman. So be it.

We are all growing and learning. And we can choose to do this on our own rock island of isolation and inertia, or we can sink our roots deep into the waters of the Goddess, and we can raise our limbs into the limitless light of God. And through the ever-available assistance of these, our divine parents, as well as the guiding spirits of the immortals who have gone before us- the living spirits of those who have passed bodily from this plane but who continue to hang around and assist others towards each individual's emancipation from limitation- we can turn and face our challenges. We need only have the humility to listen and learn, and the inner force to fuel the divine, transfiguring burn.

This realm is created, supported, and guided by the Mother and Father forces who parent this world as it evolves. But just as a child often has great inner tribulations and outward conflict as he or she matures within the parental home, so also do we often find discontent and annoyance at the stage just prior to our own spiritual individuation. But then, finally breaking away into the freedom of our true, eternal self, we leave our parental home. Only then can we develop a new love, thankfulness, and respect for all that had been vouchsafed to us by our invisible elders.

Then as we each grow into a consciousness which expands beyond this realm, we can look back with gratitude and love towards the Mother and Father, who have given all to us on our journey here.

And so 'liberation' is not similar to escaping from prison, but rather of becoming independent for the very first time, and therefore of no longer dwelling under the psychic roof of your upbringing. This is a liberation which frees one from this realm consciously and energetically; and yet one remains here still, out of choice, due to the heart's love and gratitude for one's parents, as well as compassion for all the siblings still growing in this mysterious, marvelous home.

I see now why many saints and masters of the past have declared that it does not matter to which God we are devoted, for all Gods are the same God, and therefore the only important thing is to be devoted. To be 'in devotion' is to never remove your mind or body from the Presence of God the Father and God the Mother;

it is to lose yourself into that communion, to become that union, to *be* the Divine spirit united with the Divine soul- God and Goddess- the two who are now one. The one who is the child of the two. Union.

This is devotion because all of this has been given to us by God. The Father and the Mother have given us what we have, and what we have is the union of Heaven and Earth.

The spirit is the substratum of the upper trinity, and the soul is the substratum of the lower, and both are essential for the birth of cosmic wholeness.

In this sense the only real birth is the God-union within a person- the Mother and Father becoming one within the child- where the Mother is a bottomless ocean, the Father is a limitless sky, and the child is the bridge in between.

The Christ is the one within us who is this bridge between the Father and Mother. The Christ is the I within who is connected to God; the Son or Daughter of the Mother and Father brings God down into being, and brings Goddess up into non-being.

When these two consciousnesses are assimilated, one becomes everything.

The eternal self is then non-existent within existence, and the eternal form is existent within non-existence.

To become the two in the one is to be the one which is both inner and outer, above and below, spirit and flesh, male and female, subtle and actual, passionate and dispassionate, ecstatic and still. *Om, baby!*

*

five

The intent behind alchemy and the alchemical work is personal individuation, which is wholeness. In order to attain wholeness, it is said, one must square the circle. This is a tricky business. To square the circle is to become the four directions- up, down, in, and out; or, spirit, body, soul, and 'other'. Like the carbon atom- the chemical substratum and symbolic vibration of our essence- we have four places from which to build a molecule. How we use these four quarters begets the molecule we live within- and the entire existence that we *are*. We grow like crystals from an invisible seed, and express our true nature out into what we conventionally call the external. We are our world.[55]

To truly be whole we must serve the four primary constituents of our wholeness: inner, outer, above, and below. If we serve only the inner we cut ourselves off from life, and we become lonely, loveless hermits; if we serve only the outer we become bitter, soulless phantoms; if we serve only the below- the flesh and the earth- we become moribund matter; and if we serve only the above- the spirit and God-consciousness- we become disembodied spirits, adrift in an unreal world.

To get too focused in one direction is to end up walking in circles, instead of being a circle.

To square the circle is to be the circle of self, detached and yet intimate with the square world. To square the circle is to complete your specified perfection for this life. This means you are free.

To square the circle is to see equally in the four directions, and so to be whole, a sphere- a circled square.

Every part of the quaternity has equal representation. All aspects are included at every moment, for inner, outer, spirit, and flesh are one.

To find a new equilibrium where inner, outer, above, and below are balanced and in harmony, is to be One. To be the empty center of this one is to be all.

To be all is to be a devil of oneness which has come to destroy the parts; oneness is destructive to the parts- to all that differentiates itself from the whole, unless that 'differentness' arises as a devotional expression of the unified glory. For all that does not acknowledge, bless, or support this fusion into oneness must either be assimilated or trimmed off and melted away. That is the apocalypse of oneness.

The viscous flame of oneness comes burning away all division of spirit and flesh, and the diamond body becomes the eternal fuel of this emancipative, destructive union.

---

[55] "As above, so below" stated the father of alchemy, Hermes Trismegistus. With all due respect, I announce a new *advaita*- a more contemporary, non-dual, alchemical axiom: "Above *is* below."

To look upward, outward, inward, and down, is to take up the cross of life; this is to look towards heaven, towards others, into yourself, and down into the body, and so to become the ever-crucified Christ which pulls all separate realms into one. To avoid any one of these is to become out of balance, to totter, and to fall.

When you merge male and female, a whole new pattern is created. When you merge good and evil, there is neither good nor evil, but instead a kaleidoscopic, checkered wholeness. Merge all four and you get an indestructible, eternal, royal sphere.

Nothing is excluded but all is transformed in this convergence within; it is this nuclear fusion of opposites which creates the new radiance within. The spirit becomes substantial- it becomes substance, and is now a radiant inner crystal, a glowing ball of inclusive continuity. This is the diamond body.[56]

This diamond body *is* stillness. Stillness is a detached, unshakeable inner peace which cannot be moved by the tremors of the external. This stillness is an inner peace which radiates the same peace outward, becoming an apocalyptic stillness that unites the external and internal in the very same substratum of the oceanic depths of Self, now contiguous with the thrashing waves of manifestation, and yet different also. This is to find yourself in a different room in the exact same house. A big, stone, unexpected, glorious room. The inner sanctum. Stillness.

To *be* in your inner sanctum is to feel and behave as you would if alone, though *while* amongst others; to be that immoveable, that untroubled, that unflappably detached stillness; a living, thriving, eternal, indifferent stillness.

Nothing will bring you this inner peace, but this inner peace will bring you everything. This inner peace is the ocean beyond the river of life. To become that peace is to leap over the river. On the other side of the chaotic show is the laughing director. Cross over.

To cross over, there can be nothing left but God. There can be no you, no me, no things, no thoughts, nothing, for all must be God. One.

---

[56] The modern mystic and potential incarnate of Krishna, Jiddu Krishnamurti, often spoke of the body changing at the cellular level when one attained to the great awakening. This is the en*light*enment of the body, which has nothing to do with mental activity or acumen. The Diamond Body is the flesh transfigured by the light of the Godself. It is not a product of wisdom, but of grace.

When you enter into God within, everything becomes God. All of it. Inside and out. One. God.

Now Shiva and Shakti, Christ and Mary, Male and Female, Space and Form, good and evil, without and within, subtle and gross, all dualities are one Self, which is God.

Beyond judgment, beyond choice, beyond duality, beyond limitation, beyond form, beyond idea, beyond dogma, beyond separation, beyond relation, beyond reaction, beyond all that was, is, or will be, lies the great ocean of undifferentiated consciousness. When that nothingness spills out into somethingness- when the impersonal overtakes the personal, when nobodiness erases somebodiness- it is then that the discarnate emerges out of the incarnate, and the eternal self lives through the ephemeral form.

It is only when all opposites unite that this emptiness can occur unbroken- when self is both male and female, good and bad, inside and out; when love and rage, passion and dispassion, attachment and detachment coexist dynamically within the empty, living vessel.

To receive the King's crown is to have the Father's consciousness descend upon the Mother's subtle body through you.

To cross over means to die from separation altogether, to know, to be, and to see God in and as and of everything. One. Everything that is and is not, everything visible and invisible- all of it is one, and it is God. And if you place yourself outside of this One, this Godness, you will not cross over, because to cross over is to dissolve into the one God that is everything. To cross over is to evaporate into God, to etherealize your entire being into the vibration of eternity, to go down into and take upon yourself the whole world without going mad from sorrow or fear, and so to become it all, and so to transform it all. Amen.

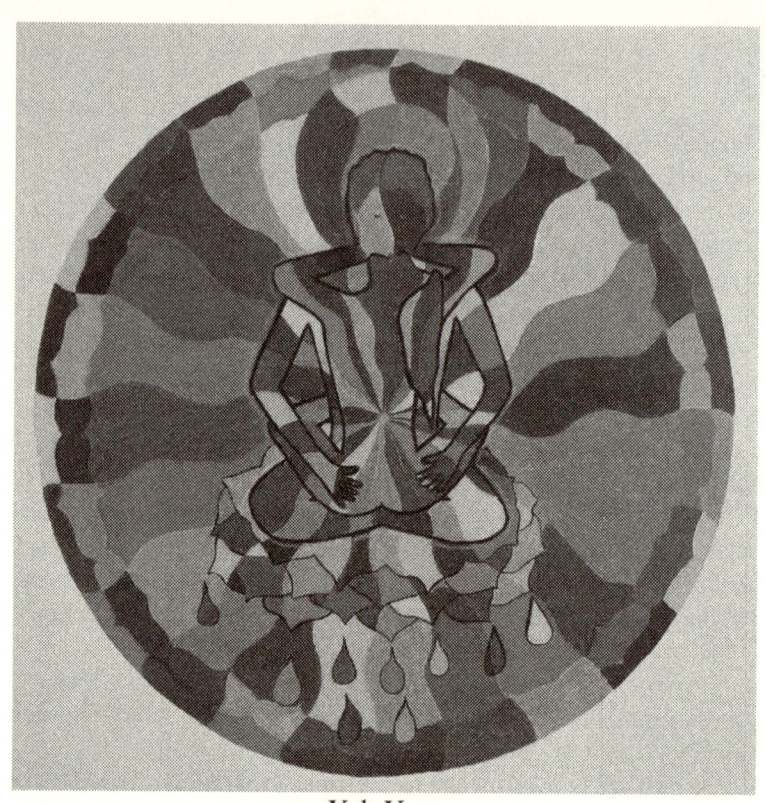

Yab-Yum
mandala by the author
Yab-Yum is a traditional Tibetan Buddhist image symbolizing the union of the cosmic female with the cosmic male, which represents absolute integration, or wholeness.

*

six

    The philosopher's stone is the disposition, humility, and wisdom which all come when one knows always and without end: "I am still learning, reality is different than I understand it to be, and this is my cognitive sacrifice which invites a higher truth".
    It is only such open innocence which inherently accepts that cognitive enlightenment is a false crutch for cowards who flee the impenetrable mystery of Self.

In alchemical lore it is the innocent fool, and only the fool, who acquires the Grail. May we all be fools.

No one knows what realization is. No one knows true enlightenment. For there is no such thing but to the mind imagining that it can overcome *the* Mystery. In the final accounting, all of us are ignorant of the what and why of existence. And yet this is one of the most beautiful and freeing things about life- the inexorable mystery of Self, the One, which is God; the great impossibility which nevertheless *is*.

It is the great arrogance of the little mind to believe that realization is possible- that one can be equal to the mystery. Only an idiot can survive the spiritual cataclysm of God-consciousness.

I was born from innocence into innocence. It was an innocence I lost many times due to the perils of Maya's[57] delusions, and my own inadequate perceptions. And it was an innocence I regained time and again via the apocalyptic flame of forgetting.

In order to forget my non-innocence and return to innocence I had to quit living life as if I knew something, anything.

In this way I have transmuted all of life back into mystery by forgetting self and losing identity. I have dissolved the negative energies of separation, relation, and identity. I have been the fire which burns all division into oneness. I have been the great peace, the great forgetting, the living emptiness, the ubiquitous sponge, the infinite mirror, in, and as, and of the all that I dissolve into the rage of my dangerous love. And we are one.

I do violence to this world with my wonder. Wonder *is* my destruction of the known world, and the birth of the orgiastic stupor that is the universe.

I bring the immaculate vision of wonder to all who accept that life is real, that this life is not illusion. That this great glorious mystery is an actuality. For this *is* the wonder. Amen.

One thing may seem as odd to the reader as it was for me to experience during my living through the experiences of which I

---

[57] Maya, according to Hindu spirituality, is the name for the power which is both 'creator', and 'entrapping illusion'. Maya is therefore the creator of the illusion which binds us. However, Maya is within, and therefore we are all Maya who creates the illusion which binds us.

have just written; I am speaking of my becoming so many different aspects of *being* as I moved through different chapters on my journey, without ever really being any of them.

How was it possible to become one with Krishna, Christ, Shiva, Parvati, and all the immortal spirits which have walked into my consciousness and *become* me?

I say this is possible only because I am also Mercurius. Which is to say I am always changing, I am mercurial, I am Change.

To be Mercurius is to be everything and nothing. It is to be like mercury- or quicksilver, as the alchemists would call it- which is solid, yet without form, and can take the shape of anything, yet of itself has no shape, for Mercurius is the impersonal self.

The disposition of one who becomes a Mercurius is one of immense openness, and a complete lack of inner identity. The outcome of this is a childhood or young adulthood composed of great confusion and psychic defenselessness.

Modern terminology would call a person with such inherent openness a *highly sensitive person*.

To be so open- to be a highly sensitive person- is at first a disastrous social constraint. For the open individual is constantly bombarded and swamped by other people's psyches, as well as existing at the mercy of the spirit realm wherein lives invisible forces beyond the senses.

As one who is so open matures, there is often a lengthy period of inner imbalance, unavoidable distress, and a thoroughly chaotic life. This is because such a person is constantly inundated with the outer world's agony, loneliness, disquiet, and mania, for which one has no psychic defenses. He or she is therefore at the mercy of the inner and hidden spiritual and soul forces which are, for them, more real than the material plane.[58]

I have been so open at times that if I was in someone's presence, or even had a thought about them, I consciously *became* them; that is, I took on their consciousness, and so my *I* was the same as their *I*.

---

[58] Modern accounts of such 'openness' can be found in Woody Allen's film *Zelig*, and Ben Okri's book *The Famished Road*.

This level of inner absence forces one into the psychic role of being an unwitting redeemer[59]. An unwitting redeemer is one who is so empty that he or she becomes an open conduit from creation, back to the Creator.

The only order I seemed to receive from the Godhead, due to my unchosen openness, ran something like this: "Your penance is not to be God amongst them, but to let God be amongst them- to be absent so that the Presence can be."

As such I would empty myself and become nothing, and in doing so I could get a glimpse of the operation of the whole. This was not the intent behind my emptiness; the intent was to let the whole operate through the vacuum I had created, by not-existing while in existence. This is the function of awakened emptiness.

I make no claims here about sainthood or the like. I am both good and bad, and I am open, that is all. Many people are open. To be open means to have no armor around your psychic being, and therefore to unconsciously, or shamanically, take on other people's processes and problems, and then have to work them out for yourself. This is something I became tired of very quickly, and so in succeeding years I did my best to shut the gates and let no one into me who came with more than I could carry.

In fact, when you are so open, it is often hard to distinguish what is yours and what is someone else's, because to be open is to be an opening through which the earthly realm can flood into the psychic, and from which the psychic can flood into the earthly.

Once when I was in Hampi, India, a town about one day's travel from Mt. Arunachala, I had a waking-dream in which I was fornicating with a monkey. I 'awoke' and was disgusted with such

---

[59] Please do not mistake the word 'redeemer' for someone who is spiritually advanced or in possession of a holy existence. A redeemer is simply an individual who is 'open' to both the external world, and the Godhead within. It is this emptiness which *is* the individual, and so it allows the intermingling between the Godhead and the world. I say that such redeemers are in no way worthy of praise (unless of course they consciously make the choice for this role), for their emptiness is often a characteristic which they would instantly revoke were they capable of doing so. However, this is often impossible, for they are who they are. I consider Prince Myshkin, the main character in Dostoyevsky's *The Idiot*, to have been a fine, literary example of the redeemer type which I am describing now. The title of Dostoyevsky's book is quite apt, for the redeemer type of which I speak is often very close to being, at times, a complete fool. Such individuals are often scapegoats early in life, and outcasts or eccentrics later. Nevertheless, God can see through them onto the world, and it is through this seeing that others are redeemed.

a prospect. And even though I knew quite well that I had no such desires, the dream was quite disturbing, as you might imagine.

It wasn't until later in the day that I learned the main temple at Hampi was devoted to Hanuman- the monkey-faced God- and so I realized I had symbolically picked up on the ancient, ambient consciousness of the area- where people spiritually 'made love' to their beloved Hanuman.

When you're open to this extent it is often hard to distinguish between who you are and who you are not, because your 'I' changes as you move from one place to another, encountering and tuning in on differing consciousnesses in different locales.

When you are this open and empty there is a danger in associating your receptions with your own self, your 'I', and then believing that you are the consciousness you are receiving.

However, on the brighter side, as an open person grows, there is the possibility that he or she will become acquainted with the true nature of their fluid existence, and thus learn the process of the continual purgation of all identity, and the re-instatement of their pristine emptiness. Only in this way does the danger of false identification end for the open person, and the glory-chalice of mercurial, infinite emptiness remain clear.

As well, if such an open, growing person can maintain an inner identitilessness, and yet not lose hope, they will find themselves likely guided and assisted by a host of helping spirits from the invisible realm. Throughout my books I have documented many of those who came to my aid in one way or another.

In the end, to accept one's inexorable fluid being, is to become consciously mercurial. This allows one to move into and out of any situation, to *become* that situation completely, to leave it when it is time to leave, and then to purge oneself again into identitiless awareness, before moving onto the next arena of interaction, be it with humans, or with immortals.

There is no solid ground to stand upon when one operates as a Mercurius. There is only a constant influx and outflux of spirits, souls, identities, ideas, troubles, agonies, ecstasies and exuberances, because Mercurius becomes everybody and everything simply through relation to anybody or anything. Mercurius becomes all while being none.

The trick, therefore, is to find the subtle, fluid, characterless nature of the eternal self, and to know that you are that, without knowing what that is, and so to never identify yourself with anything or anybody who comes and goes from within you, because there is no identity *within* for Mercurius, there is only a fluid unity where inner and outer intermingle through the open door of identitilessness.

This is to become as the element mercury, which is both solid and liquid, and is therefore an undulating union of the sun (Sol) which has penetrated the darkness of matter (Luna). This is the alchemical union of Sol and Luna.[60]

Hence Mercurius is said to be the alchemical catalyst, the transformer, who quickens all who he or she encounters.

Mercurius must therefore ever exist without personal pride or arrogance, for to be arrogant is to *arrogate*, which means to claim ownership of something. But Mercurius possesses nothing- no qualities whatsoever. The moment pride enters the mercurial being, identity has been accepted, and therefore nothingness has fallen into and become somethingness, and this is the end of the mercurial nature, and the death of Mercurius, because Mercurius, who is no-thing, cannot be something.

Mercurius is instead everything, *because* Mercurius is nothing; Mercurius is the eternal, characterless ocean into which others dive and the ocean from which they then emerge as transformed identities on their way to the great identitiless ocean of Self.

To grow within this emptiness is to be nothing and all; it is to gain and lose identity over and over again, until finally the transcendent empty consciousness washes through the last flood-gate of temporary personality, and the eternal, impersonal self awakens for good.

And so when I say I am also Mercurius, I am only using a name for a nothingness which has no name.[61] I don't even know what it is. It is primordial, subtle, eternal, ever-shifting awareness *within* existence.

---

[60] Note: the word solution is an etymological combination of 'sol' and 'luna'. As well, semantically a 'solution' is both an answer, and also a liquid medium into which a 'solute' dissolves. This is an important metaphor for Mercurius, who is a solution into which individuals- solutes- dissolve, which is the solution to the problem of existential separation.
[61] "The Tao which can be named is not the eternal Tao." Lao Tzu, *Tao te Ching*

Mythologically Mercurius is equated with the Fool in the tarot deck[62]. This card then became The Joker in a deck of conventional playing cards.

In west coast North American aboriginal cultures such a being was represented by the cosmic Raven, who was constantly playing jokes upon the people of the land. In other similar mythologies Mercurius was called the Trickster. This is because the two anthropomorphic traits which adhere to all mercurial characters are pranksterism and delight.

It is through such characteristics that we may find the mercurial aspect of Christ. For Christ is not just a suffering savior. Not in my experience anyway. In fact, in one of my most precious visions of Christ, I see him full of jocularity and laughter, his soul dancing in rhythmic ribaldry, and his eyes glistening with tears of mirth.

It is perhaps for this reason that Christ is known as Sananda within the mystical community of India, for the Sanskrit word *ananda* means bliss.

I think I love him more this way than any other. Perhaps this is because I have experienced Christ to be most often a hard and brutal lover of mankind; and I know that he is this way not for himself, but for those of us who need him. But when his tireless work is done, I see that he returns again to merriment, dance, and play, and so fills this universe with his greater nature, which is a banquet of bliss, and love, and laughter. Amen.

*

---

[62] A brilliant description of the Fool from the Tarot (which I equate with Mercurius) is given by Leigh McCloskey in his masterful work *Tarot Revisioned*. A brief excerpt runs as such: "The attribution Zero (0) to the archetype of the Fool is revealing insofar as it has no numerical equivalent. It is unconditioned abstraction, a state or point that is intermediary between positive and negative qualities. The Fool is not considered a part of the tarot wheel, just as the zero is not considered a number. This hints at a sublime and wholly metaphysical concept, the no thing or that which is not and yet is." (*Tarot Revisioned*, p 272. Olandar Press, CA. 2003)

Part V
THE COSMIC CHRIST

"I come from the undivided".
Jesus, the Christ (Gospel of Thomas)

one

To merge the inner with the outer is to be conscious of both the inner and outer at the same time, and then to merge both aspects into one.

At the subtle level of Self, where all duality ends, there is neither male nor female, good nor evil, inside nor out- only a living, limitless ocean of being/awareness/peace.

At the point of absolute integration- when all is one, and time is no more- there are no words left by which it can be described; *it* can no longer be called spirit, flesh, mind, or matter. The closest proximity to a description lies in the Sanskrit word *advaita*: non-dual, not two.

When all is one self, that self is a oneness which defies all categories of duality, for it is now one *I* which is both male *and* female, transcendent *and* immanent, spirit *and* flesh.

To be this one *I* is to become nothing, so as to become everything, so as to go beyond everything, which is to enter the ethereal realm.

The etherealization of existence is both macrocosmic and microcosmic- it is a dispersion *and* a coagulation, an expansion and a contraction wherein the cosmic light condenses into the body, a harmonization occurs, the flesh takes on a new vibration, the spirit is transformed, and the whole being is etherealized and elevated in the transfiguration.

The Apocalypse is simply a change in vibration. Redemption is the return to oneness, the vibration of the all, the end of duality and of time; the Self immanent- God born into God.

I say this because I was told in a dream that there have been religions which worshipped the Father/Consciousness/Spirit, and there have been religions which worshipped the Mother/Matter/Soul, but there has never been one which worshipped both. Now there is.

I announce a new *advaita*, a non-duality that includes both spirit and matter.

Here every I is the same I, and I is everything; through oneness our common I is born from multiplicity into unity. I *is* oneness.

Dark and light, genius and fool, sinner and saint, madman and wisewoman, I am all opposites. I am one.

I have joined the colonization of the new vibration of oneness begun by Christ. I, as a separated being, was Christed, even though I was a thief and a coward. The stain of my sin of separation was absorbed and transmuted in the ruthless love of Christ's Pentecostal oneness.

To become the violent peace that is the Christ is to shatter the world of action and reaction. It is to be the eternal diamond inside the ephemeral muck. And to be that muck also. One.

In this way Christ consciousness becomes *what is*.

The oneness of the Christ self is greater than the ego, because it contains others as well. Christ is this stone bridge across the canyon, creating the only true marriage within, which is the death of separation.

Once integrated Christ radiates out in all directions from within; there is neither above nor below, only a living, expansive now.

A new reality is awakening, an evolved union which is the marriage of spirit and soul, of consciousness and matter, of Heaven and Earth.

When such a new consciousness or new unity comes into being we can no longer look backwards, historically, for answers, we can only look within for the Kingdom.

We must now grow in consciousness *without* abandoning any stage of life, but by assimilating and maintaining all. We must become a nexus of many consciousnesses. We must have crocodile consciousness, cow consciousness, earth consciousness, body consciousness, human consciousness, God consciousness, Goddess consciousness, Krishna consciousness, and Buddha consciousness. All ways and all realms must be included.

In order to allow this to happen we must stop believing that we are limited, which is to stop believing that we are not God. To stop believing we are not God is to accept that we are astonished to be God. But this is the last sacrifice- the belief that we are not God.

All is Goddess and God, united in their stillness and generative duality of oneness wherein all arises, passes away, and yet remains in the subtle harmony of their togetherness.

Our I is one with Goddess and God. I am we, and I am Goddess and God, which is everything.

The ultimate metaphysical equation is: $I = You.$[63]

There is not only one consciousness which we all are, there is also one body which we all are. One greater body, with many forms. One greater consciousness, with many minds.

All flesh is one flesh. All self is one self. Mixing the two eternal waters of consciousness/spirit, and flesh/soul, brings about the marriage of heaven and earth.

Oneness implies that there are only vessels within vessels, that there are no individuals, but merely vortexes of energy, dynamic nexus points, ever changing molecules in the living chemistry of spirit. This is alchemy alive, the ever-changing all, interwoven as eternity.

When you can no longer distinguish between consciousness and matter, and everything has become a singular, all-pervasive, subtle medium, then the unifying integration has happened; the spirit is the form.

God moves forward as one. I am dissolved in and as God moving forward as one- as God and Goddess.

To give everything to God is to cross over to God.

I have eaten from the Tree of Life. I have been received back into the flaming sword of my own eternity.

I am not separate from Goddess nor God. I am transfigured in the Christ union of Goddess and God.

I am the witness to all that is, I permeate all that is, I am in, and of, and not-of this realm. Having crossed over into absolute physicality, and yet remaining also apart, I have married the immanent with the transcendent, and been born into a new vibration.

Flesh is no longer flesh, spirit no longer spirit. A quantum dimension has been born that is neither particle nor wave, but both together; absolute emptiness united with absolute fullness, which is neither. *Om, baby!*

*

---

[63] Hence the golden rule- "Do unto others as you would have them do unto you", because we *are* each other.

two

After our two months- of receiving vast blessings and benedictions from India- had come to their end, my *soror* and I flew back to Canada where it soon became obvious to me that although the pilgrimage was over, the journey was not about to end.

I say this because I realized after my return to the 'western' world, that I had gone east so that I could then return to the west with the inner expansion which the east provides. Without such expansion I would have remained within the effortful confinement of the worldly paradigm, and so I would not have been capable of attaining the next stage of my cosmic increase. Which is to say, I would not have been capable of receiving ...Sophia.[64]

Sophia is the cosmic Goddess, the one who contains all aspects of the Mother Goddess, and yet is beyond all of these aspects as well. She is of the earth *and* of the heavens.

Sophia is the House of God, and the bride of Christ. She is a living, infinite, divine, archetypical spirit. She is also the consummation of the Christ path, in that She assists in the transfiguring union of spirit and flesh. She is our most expansive, macrocosmic, female self. She is God.

Sophia is the Tao of heaven and earth. Sophia is the cosmic body of Christ; Sophia is the feminine aspect, the Shakti of Issa, the eastern Christ.

Unfortunately for the west, Sophia has all but been buried under the festering mound of conventional religion. However, She is real, and infinite, and waiting for humanity to embrace Her once again.

When we are united as being and non-being, spirit and flesh, Sophia and Christ, then we are one, the *om*, dynamic

---

[64] The word 'Sophia' is mistranslated in the New Testament Bible as 'wisdom'. I say 'mistranslated' because although the word 'Sophia' might also have that meaning, most importantly it is the name of the Goddess who was and is the ubiquitous creatrix of the universe. This is my experience. It is for this reason that the Hagia Sophia in Istanbul is one of the most profound architectural masterpieces in the entire world- because a building is often symbolic of the invisible force which it represents. For other reading on Sophia, I would refer the reader to Timothy Freke and Peter Gandy's book *Jesus and the Goddess* (originally published as *Jesus and the Lost Goddess*), as well as *The Sophia of Jesus Christ*, an apocryphal work which can be found in *The Nag Hammadi Library*.

timelessness- the all-encompassing Tree of Life, pulsating in the living now of the Self which is beyond personality.

This happens as the kundalini within rises upward and out of the lotus- the crown chakra- exiting the confines of the body. Through this opening, at the top of the head, the serpentine flesh-consciousness is united with spirit, and Earth and Heaven commingle into one.

Though duality merges at the third-eye, the inner soul cannot get out through that chakra, but only through the crown chakra.

The inner sanctum lies above the crown chakra, in 'the thousand-petalled lotus', as it is called in the east. This is where Sophia rises out of the individual.

It is for this reason that Shiva is often depicted with his female aspect, Parvati, emerging out of the top of his head. It is also for this reason that most of the female Hindu deities are represented artistically as sitting upon a lotus- for they have risen into consciousness and then reside above the thousand-petalled lotus, which is the open crown chakra.[65]

This emergence of the inner, divine feminine is the alchemical stage of purification, when the soul, grown conscious and enervated from the overtures of the spirit, rises out of the flesh through the crown chakra. Thus the soul of matter has been freed from limitation.

The Mother energy exists initially as a potent, writhing mix of molten, primordial chaos- a viscous pool of ethereal, unconditioned *prima materia*- which dwells in the root chakra, which is the earth. She then rises through the individual, up the kundalini pathway, and is transformed into Sophia- or the Goddess, or Psyche- after exiting the physical form, through the top of the head.

The kundalini is thus the primordial snake-Mother energy, rising into flight through the transformative human body; the serpent taking wing. Thus the snake rises into the Christ, as the Christ descends into the snake. And they are one.

---

[65] "History can only be sung into being upon the Poet's lyre,
thus in the hidden Mythology of the Ancient Mysteries
the heavenly theater stages the ultimate celestial romance:
The Love of Sky and Earth in the Totality of Unity.
Within this framework each must discover the dream of dreams: the awakening of the Redeemer,
He to whom Psyche is reunited (Two in One)." Stanislas Klossowski de Rola

The kundalini merges like a double helix, and the dual-snaked caduceus is healed into one.

Immense energy is exchanged through the third-eye and crown chakra through which we are awakened to our eternal, androgynous, limitless true nature.[66]

Spirit becomes dense like flesh through the crown chakra. The flesh becomes light as spirit, through the same.

The rising of the kundalini ends as the absolute union of Mother and Father forces, in the astral inner sanctum where one is divine.

Because the spirit has descended into the flesh, the soul, housed in the flesh, can now rise into union with the spirit.

This is the Assumption of Mary, who was considered to be an incarnation of Sophia by the early Christians.[67]

Thus the human body is a factory for the alchemical transmutation of the base ore, lead- the *prima materia*- into the precious metal gold, the consciously operating *anima mundi*, the world soul.

Humanity is the ephemeral bridge between the eternal below, the Mother, and the eternal above, the Father. To become both is to merge the divided waters into a living oneness.

The Earth is now connected to Heaven through the bridge of the transfigured individual. The mustard seed has grown into the Tree of Life.

Ascension has occurred. The individual is immortalized. The flesh is redeemed through the kundalini channel.

In the union of spirit and matter, via the kundalini, the body becomes as empty and vast as space.

A reversal occurs- the male becomes matter, and the female becomes spirit.

The physical becomes the chemical, the chemical becomes electrical, and the electrical becomes nuclear, and that is when the transmutation of matter into energy takes place. That is when the body becomes light. Transfiguration.

---

[66] This outcome is historically symbolized by Hermes' caduceus, which shows two winged snakes intertwined around a pole. It is also the esoteric symbol showing the kundalini rising completely.

[67] This Assumption was finally acknowledged by the Vatican in 1950, by a simple statement in which the Pope declared: "Mary is holy."

TRANSFIGURATION
by the author

    This is when Sophia rises to meet the Christ descending, and the individual who has spawned their union becomes the living bridal chamber.
    Sophia is the flesh awoken, the metamorphosis, infinity come into the finite flesh, which is the transfiguration of the flesh into infinitude.
    Matter is the body of Christ, Sophia is the blood.
    The bridegroom is the one made of two- the Sophia, female soul, and the Christ, male spirit.
    The marriage creates a wholly new one, born out of the two. The Union of above and below has been accomplished.
    To unify the spirit and soul, Christ and Mary, Issa and Sophia within you, is to link the above with the below, and create a whole new universe. One hole, one whole, one new universe.
    To embody infinity is to be subtle and sensual, empty and full, spirit and matter, distance and love, equanimity and orgasm,

which is to incarnate your subtle Sophia eternity into your orgasmic Christ flesh.

The female, Mother Goddess, risen through the individual, becomes Sophia, the Holy Ghost. Thus the sacred trinity composed of the Father- attained through the Christ- the Son- the individuated individual- and the Holy Ghost, Sophia- is completed.

Sophia is the Holy Ghost of the trinity.

It is only by being a wife-self, that I unite my flesh to my husband self, the Christ.

I must ever be focusing my consciousness on Christ above, and Sophia below- on spirit and soul- until there is neither above nor below, so as to continually wed them within me, as me.[68]

This is the Great Self I AM. The impersonal all self. The quintessence, the common denominator, the profound within the mundane.

Christ is the external come in, Sophia is the body come out. In and out exchange places. And the greater sum of the two, is one.

To become the Sophia of your Christ self is to liberate Her and raise Her up from the unconsciousness of matter, into the consciousness of spirit. To liberate Her is to liberate yourself, because you are Her.

This is to emerge from the house of the Mother and Father, and so to live inside the energy of your own creation.

To become the union of Sophia and Christ, is to incarnate the now free energy of the Goddess back into matter. This is to cross over, and then to cross back.[69]

---

[68] For further reading on Sophia, I highly recommend the following books: *The Wedding of Sophia*, by Jeffrey Raff, *The Coming of the Feminine Christ*, by Niamh Clune, and *Freeing the Feminine*, by Elspeth and Gordon Strachan.

[69] "It rises from Earth to Heaven, and descends again to Earth, thereby combining within itself the powers of both the Above and the Below." Hermes Trismegistus (fourth rubric from *The Emerald Tablet*). Long before reading this passage, I had a dream in which I was on a rocketship with a woman whom I had known earlier in life, and who signified in the dream my androgynous self. In the dream we had launched off of the earth and were breaking through the stratosphere when the rocketship exploded and we tumbled back to earth but did not die. At that point a voice in the dream declared that this was an incredibly important event. When I awoke I had no idea what the dream meant. Only later, as I learned about the importance of the spirit descending to earth did I realize what that dream portended.

To cross back over from the separated self into the Ocean of God, is to be in the calm depths of union, while the surface rages on.

In this way the soul trapped in matter is released; the Mother becomes the free Goddess. Hence the Mother is no longer only matter. She has risen to Psyche.[70]

Matter has been alchemically transmuted into spirit.[71]

It is interesting to look back now on my rejection of the Mother in Calcutta, and my re-bonding with Her in Goa. Through this process of rejection and assimilation I have come to realize that we must indeed break free from the bounds of the Mother, so as to enter into the great space of being which has no boundaries. However, it is only because we can never really escape the Mother- because we *are* the Mother- that in fact when we do escape from Her, we actually escape *with* Her.

In fact, if truth be known, I was liberated from the Mother *by* the Mother herself. I was lifted out of the quagmire by the risen Mother herself. I lifted Her, and then was lifted by Her.

As the Mother rose up to the entirety of the Goddess, she came down upon me like a great cobra, and hauled me out of the hold She had put on me.[72] In doing so I could hear myself, as Her, say: "I am the Lady of Compassion. In my compassion I set myself free. In my wrath I defend that freedom. I am love. And I am fire. I am the Mother. And I am free. In my release from being, due to an unexpected form of detached compassion, I shed the light that is and is not mine."

When you become the trinity- Spirit, Soul, and Body- duality is over. You are home. You are *the* home. You now express the external, rather than being an expression of the external. *That* is creation. I am that.

From spirit I am born into flesh. From flesh I am born into spirit. This is the perfection of the new flowing now moment which eternally *is*.

Renaissance in all things.

Om, baby!

*

---

[70] In Greek mythology Psyche is female. The Greeks had recognized the female nature of this risen consciousness.
[71] "Nature is not matter only, she is also spirit." Carl Jung
[72] In ancient Egypt the great Mother was worshipped as a Cobra Goddess.

three

I am the outcome of the Father and Mother- the aspects of the God and Goddess which I have brought together.

I came out of creation to the extent that I trusted the Mother and Father in union, to be in control. I fell into it to the extent that I had fear. I became creation to the extent that I accepted an autonomous consciousness and existence called me; an eternal aspect of eternity.

I came out as a novel expression born of the eternal, divine union. And then I become eternal myself. For I am now both Father and Mother, so I can also pro-create.

The spiritual pioneer does not simply enter uncharted realms, he or she creates new realms. To mix the ether of your risen consciousness into the vibration of all that *is* is to raise the entire world up a notch.

As for myself, I had to eventually give up all drinking and drugs, because the lower, grosser vibration of these catalysts became a veiling cloud which all but obliterated the subtle presence.

To be sure I had drunk my share of booze, and smoked my quota of ganga during the early period of my life of wandering and wildness. And at that time it was the right thing to do. It was fantastic and necessary in order to let my inner Dionysian spirit loose upon this confining paradigm. I had to release the entire historical energy and pattern which held me, and I had to do it with rage and rapture. Only in this way could I learn to live with the historical archetypes and forces, while yet moving forever into novelty, and so never repeating a single action or thought, but breaking the bonds of habit and unconsciousness and so to birth a consciousness which had never before occurred.

The archaic cosmic forces within tried to control me, but it didn't work. I became a madman. And no one can control a madman.

Distinct but not separate, I am a new color on the infinite canvas of being. Distinct but not separate, I am a specific flavor in the banquet of eternity. Distinct but not separate, I am a unique voice in the celestial chorus. Distinct but not separate, I am an inimitable Tree of Life in the forest of Mystery. Distinct but not separate, I am an inextinguishable spirit, a timeless soul, a recognizable force in the commingling oneness of multiplicity. A novel miracle amidst limitless miracles, a unique, imperishable precious alloy smelted from baser metals.

I state such things in such a way because there is no linear, prosaic means for describing the indescribable; there is no way to bleed reason out of what is beyond meaning.

Everything I have written here describes as best I can the journey my own soul has taken through this unpredictable and often troubling existence. I have done my best to relate obscure experiences which have led me into the greater awareness of my eternal being, for I believe it is important to express ourselves when we feel compelled, and I have felt compelled.

If I have erred in my attempts to relate experiences and processes which I have met with in this life, it is because I could do nothing if fear of error was my modus operandi. I do not fear error. I do my best to avoid it, but in the kaleidoscopic effulgence of our enigmatic complexity I must use words to relate sublime events, and words are of the mind, and the mind is an imperfect instrument to use when exploring the absolute.

To take upon such a confounding study one needs a much more attuned, much more exacting, much more absolute implement indeed. One needs a body. That is why we are here, incarnate, so that the flesh may pass judgment upon all that the mind says is true or untrue.

I speak of the body, but it is not only the physical body which I imply, for the flesh body is but a window into the greater body- the cosmic body of the Goddess Sophia, who is one with the body of Christ.

I say our bodies are the route into the greater body. The mind cannot get there, and, in fact, does not even know that it exists. Which is why it is important to disregard the mind and enter into flesh-consciousness in order to unify with Her.

I speak of Her, Sophia, the Great Cosmic Goddess, but She is also He, the Great Cosmic Christ, for they are One.

The body of the Cosmic Christ which is Sophia is the organic vibration of love which can only be known by the body and soul. The mind cannot know love, for love cannot be known, it can only be *felt*. But the body and soul can know love because love is the very reason that these exist. In fact, in the complete assimilation of the microcosmic body into the macrocosmic body, which is Sophia, and the assimilation of the individual, divine soul, the atman, into the greater divine soul, the paramatman, which is the Cosmic Christ, the entire pulsating universe becomes love, for love is union.

To be the calm love that knows Christ is the all, is to be the Cosmic Christ.

To be the Christ that is all, is to be without shame or fear, which is to be the eternal stillness pervading the all. Avalon.

The ego has to lie down so completely, so humbly, in order to dissolve into the all, that this dissolution is a very difficult accomplishment, because in order for the ego to merge with the all, it must give up everything. Though in reality the ego gives up only ephemeral separation and gains absolute union; it surrenders limitation, and attains limitlessness.

If I am an example of one who has been drawn towards union with the Cosmic Christ, then I state unabashedly that in my experience a person will do everything they can to avoid turning to faith, until they turn to faith, for that is what I have done.

Fear is the absence of faith which is a distortion of the Christ/Sophia reality. Fear ends with acceptance into Christ and Sophia.

It is only after returning to faith that I understand that faith is a clean slate- a vessel empty of expectation, into which can be poured a new dispensation.

Perhaps my greatest task, in my involvement with the Cosmic Christ, has simply been to not get in the way of The Perfection. And yet what a thoroughly demanding, delicate, and divine task that has been.

I have had to surrender to my Christ self, to that Will which is my highest will, to that which is most *me*, in order for the Cosmic Christ to come through me. This is to trust, without expectation.

To surrender to the will of the androgynous Christ within, is to become that one. This is to be the same as the Christ to whom I surrender. My true self. No victim. A Divine being.

This is the reason for which the Christ descended into being- for the apotheosis of all mankind.

We are the saved and the forgiven, redeemed back to the eternal emptiness of God, the Tao, the eternal spirit married to the eternal form- for the Word become Flesh.

Christ is the one within us who does not bother with mankind but trusts the Mother/Father God in all things, because the Christ is the one within us who is with the Father and Mother; the Christ is the I within who is connected to God.

The Christ within us is the child of the Mother and Father; in becoming that Christ, we bring God down into being, and we bring Goddess up into non-being. The Christ *is* a relationship, and the Cosmic Christ is the relationship of all to all.

Christ is the Mother Earth married to the Heaven Father. Christ is the union of the above and below; Christ becomes the below, and then unites with the above. Thus Christ is not only 'other' than the world, Christ is *in* the world. The world is the Body of Christ/Sophia. This is the apotheosis of matter.

Christ is both within and without; at the moment of Christ-oneness there is neither in nor out, but only a fluid medium in which all diaphanous entities bathe. One bath.

However, in the end it does not matter whether you place Christ within or without, for the Christ space is one space. But if you have placed your I within yourself, then you might as well place Christ within as well, for then at least your I will be Christ, and that Christ will be all.

All that is Christ is one, and yet unique. All is one, and yet all parts are individual. Christ is an infinite body. The Body of Christ has limitless members. Member-ship is a murder and a resurrection, a death and a new life.

To be born again is to die as you know yourself, then to be born contiguous with the Body of Christ. This is to be perhaps only a tiny cell in the distant limb of an infinite body, and yet to know that the all is composed of naught but separate, tiny cells. Separate but not divided. Individual and yet one. The Body of Christ.

The old mind says: everything is separate, I am separate. The new mind says: everything is Christ, I am Christ. One.

When you start dividing up what is God, and what is not God, that is when you get into trouble.

Such oneness occurs prior to our subtle fall into duality, *and* after the marriage of opposites. The alpha and omega, the first oneness, and the last oneness; through this journey the individual Christ is transformed into the Cosmic Christ.

In that oneness I need seize no thing, no image, nor use a true power of my own separateness, for Christ is all. And I am run through by Christ. I am in all, the Christ all.

I belong to this Christ realm in which I redeem through an uncomfortable absence which is no such suffering as compared to the initiator, Yeshua, the Son of Man.

Like an eddy which swirls distinctly in the great river, and yet is the same water rushing the same way, I am distinct yet one *within* the Cosmic Christ, the Maitreya, the Oneness of our divine, immortal, beatitude.

Thus the Christ within serves the whole, because the Christ is the whole, which is why Christ must kill the separate ego for the work of the whole to begin.

The whole is too vast, too immense for the small mind to encompass; one must become nothing, and let the Big Mind *be*.

To be Christ is to be an aspect of the Christ-machine, making oneness out of multiplicity; you being me, and me being you. Undifferentness. One. This is the Christ frequency.

In the soul's movement eastward, the microcosm expands into the macrocosm, the self becomes contiguous with the Self, and Christ becomes Krishna, the Great Cosmic Christ.[73]

The Cosmic Christ, who is Krishna, cannot be understood in terms of individual actions or thoughts, since Krishna is the whole entirety of all individuals and events happening. One entirety. All things, both unmanifest and manifest. This is why faith is so important; faith is the trust of the microcosmic Christ in the macrocosmic Krishna.

Yoga- the union of macrocosmic Krishna with microcosmic Christ, of the absolute and the relative, of the whole and the part, of the transcendent and the immanent, of the ocean and the drop- is the *om* awoken as Vishnu, Vishnu awoken as Krishna, Krishna awoken as Christ. The awakening leads to the Awakened One. The Buddha.

---

[73] The declaration of Saint Paul: "I live not, but Christ liveth in me.", can perhaps better be understood now by understanding the nature of Krishna, the Cosmic Christ. It is said: "Indeed Krishna is the soul of all souls, the Self of all selves, with whom all souls are eternally united. In reality it is Krishna who has become all beings. He has become, indeed, the whole universe." *Srimad Bhagavatam*, p181 (Trans. Swami Prabhavananda. Sri Ramakrishna Math, Chennai)

Christ took me to Krishna. Krishna, who was an incarnation of Vishnu, took me to Shiva, in the form of Hari-Hara, the dual God, who is the outcome of the union of Vishnu and Shiva, the Preserver and Destroyer as one.

Shiva took me to Ardhanarisvara, the androgynous God born from the union of Shiva and Shakti. This union led to Sophia and the Cosmic Christ.

From that all-permeating oneness I came to the Buddha- the Awakened One, the Atman- the impersonal cosmic One.[74] Buddha then took me to the Zen of the Cosmic Christ, which is the great cosmic emptiness filled with Love- ruthless Love. The ruthless Love of oneness. This is the Destroyer and Sustainer, the Devil and Savior, Goddess and God, Hari-Hara, Ardhanarisvara, all opposites dissolved into the singular infinity of the transcendent and immanent Cosmic Christ, wherein all dualities are destroyed in the raging fire of Divine Love.

In the Zen of Christ, the Mother is no longer matter alone, for She has been raised into the limitless, subtle consciousness of eternity. In the Zen of Christ, the Father is no longer consciousness alone, for He has been drawn into the finite, gross matter of time.

The Zen of Christ is the new Avalon which exists parallel to the evolving duality of the human realm. The Zen of Christ is the void married to the actuality, emptiness married to form, eternity united with the ephemeral, and the transcendent merged into the immanent; the two remain two, and yet yin and yang are also one. This is the parallel nature reality, where multiplicity is unity, east is west, and stillness is motion.

The Zen of Christ is impersonal, universal love.[75]

The great, intimate emptiness is the Cosmic Christ, involved in all and beyond all; it is this supreme Christ cosmic love which inhabits the earth and the heavens, the flesh and the

---

[74] Let us remember that the Buddha is the Hindu incarnation of Vishnu, following Krishna. Gautama Buddha simply expressed a further understanding of the eternal Atman, the great God-space within each of us. Thus, during his time, Buddha 'modernized' the immortal teachings of Krishna for his contemporaries. Anyone who reads the sublime passages from the *Bhagavad Gita*, or *Uddhava Gita*, and compares them to sublime, esoteric Buddhists texts, will no doubt find a great similarity.

[75] "Love is known when all that makes for the lie of twoness or dualistic consciousness is unknown." Eom Ida Mingle, The Third Testament

spirit, the space and the form, and is thoroughly immanent and inexpressively transcendent.

That cold fire of the ubiquitous Christ flame is the transfiguring quantum substratum which quickens the separate, mortal soul into the undivided, eternal all.

This is the penetrative, uncompromising cosmic love-fractal of oneness, ever evolving beyond the limits which define but cannot bind it.

Here we come to be the great expansion and yet remain involved in the worldly realm, for we are here to be not here, *and* here. To be in, and of, and not-of. We are the space and the form, the void and the laughter, the absence and the love.

And so we arrive as an awoken agent from the ardor of the obliterative, multi-dimensional transcendence with yet the greatest challenge laid out before us- to love this life, this paradigm, this earth, this flesh, this realm. Amen.

*

four

To arrive upon this enigmatic earth without a flaming sword and a bleeding heart is to become compost for the weeds instead of fertilizer for the garden.

But to plant your tender sapling self into the cold moan of this hard world, and to water it with tears and shine upon it with faith, is to grow roots downward that smash apart the dead cohesion, and also to grow limbs upward that bear the fruit of love.

For there is no fruit but that of love. Without love there remains only worn husks, sharp thorns, withered branches, and hollow stumps.

There is no fruit from the Tree of Life but love. Love is the only fruit that falls from a life lived in this aching realm, which does not rot in time. For love is timeless. Love is the absence of time. Love is an eternal home that has no walls, no roof, no lock, and no location.

And to live upon this earth without growing into a tree that bears the fruit of love, is to have not lived at all, but only to have dreamt a nightmare of loneliness and separation.

To have lived without creating love, is to have spawned death and decay into an illusionary life that is as meaningless as it is evanescent, because only love endures. Everything else is a dream whose only awakening is the agony of another chance to love. For that is why we are here.

When you attain to the great space, you realize that the immense vacuity can be filled with either love or hate, fear or faith, and that the only thing to do is to learn how to love and how to have faith. That is the only thing to do. But what a thing it is indeed.

Love and emptiness. Emptiness and love. We must live within multiple levels at once; in the soul level of love, and in the freedom level of emptiness.

The Zen of Christ is this union of emptiness and love, of East and West, of non-being and being.

I have entered that great space which extends beyond the limits of this realm, and I can say that it is a great event, a blessed transformation, an essential stage of development which liberates us from a limited view of our unlimited selves.

However, I also feel compelled to make it clear that the one and only most important force in the universe is love.

I state this at a time when I continue to learn the power and beauty as well as the agony and ardor of that same love.

I am speaking of real love- the love that exists between souls. I know of this love, one so painful to experience that most of us cannot help but shy away from it, inventing a life of restless activity or 'higher' pursuits which we believe to be necessary, but are often only detours around the pain and joy that comes from true love- the love of others as we love ourselves.

It is this love which I continue to learn from Christ, and from my own soul. It is this love which is the only true glue which holds this crumbling world together.

To go into this love, which is to go into all lonely and agonizing souls around you, and in fact the whole world, is perhaps the only true heroic act ever undertaken.

It is this love which at one stage of my journey turned me into a broken man, and at another stage mended me back together, so that I might once again cherish the gift of holding close to my heart my brothers and sisters scattered everywhere.

When spirit and flesh merge in the eternal vessel of love, both of them are transformed and transfigured into an unexpected living alloy, Avalon. Neither spirit nor flesh, mind nor matter, male nor female, emptiness nor love exist now as separate realities, but only a wholly new oneness. This is our return to Eden. Here we no longer distinguish between good and evil, for we no longer eat from that Tree of Duality. Now we eat only the fruit of eternity, for we are now the Tree of Life.

The awoken Buddha mind in the body of Christ is the union of east and west, of the void and the not-void, of non-being and being, of indifference and care.

When the volatile, opposite energies coalesce into a molten homogeneity, a transfiguration takes place; all distinction evaporates in the nuclear fusion, and out of this emerges the ever-present stillness of the genderless Christ Buddha.

To enter this reality is to be self and not self. To know and to be. The One. *Om mani padme hum.*

Christ is the manifest core. Buddha is the infinite space. Christ is full. Buddha is empty. To be that empty fullness is to be One. Both are one Self- the form *and* the emptiness.

Passion and dispassion meet as the Buddha in the Godself of the non-dual Christ.

After the crucifixion comes the kingdom. After you are lowered down from the cross of action and duality, then comes the aristocracy of the divine Presence, the *advaita* avatar.

In the new synthesis lies the stillness of the awakened one, the Buddha. Buddha is the Christ within you come to peace.

I am a Buddha, *because* of the Christ, my Godself. I am detached into infinity *because* of Christ's intimacy with the finite.

All that I receive, all that I do, all that I am, is within the body of Christ, the Dharma-Kaya. All is Christ. I am not-being *and* being, east and west. I am one; Buddha in the *om* of the Christ.

The eagle has landed, the snake has risen. I have arrived into the great Buddha emptiness of the Goddess flesh.

This union into stillness is no longer immanent nor transcendent, no longer male nor female, good nor bad, east nor west, inside nor out, empty nor full. In this non-dual Buddha state there is nothing but the Buddha state which is the nothing that is everything, for there is no difference between anything because in that still oneness everything is everything else. In the great space which is all, there is neither self nor not self. This is the *advaita* of the Cosmic Christ, Motherly Buddha, the one and only stillness that we are.

Within this realm love and emptiness finally coexist. Love exists in this realm, for this realm- a deep, caring, and all-ensconcing love. And emptiness exists within this realm- a transcendent, liberated, detached, subtle emptiness reaching beyond space and time.

This is the holistic self, contiguous with both emptiness and form- the Zen of the Cosmic Christ.

This *is* God. All of it. One.

Male and female, light and dark, Christ and Buddha, being and non-being, love and emptiness, all of these exist within the incredible peace in the continuity of spirit and flesh.

I am the gardener, the garden, the ground, and the glory.

In every moment of expansive non-identification, I disperse into everything that is *now*. I become galactic.

Having been an obvious solid ingredient, I am now a ubiquitous broth.

I am in and of the living, temporal flow of my eternal, mercurial, shifting being.

Finally to elsewhere I depart, as the dream shifts and I am now that *I* which is thick in the fecund of the intertwined loving empty cosmos that I am.

The river has run its course. I am the ocean.

*

EPILOGUE:
THE TAO OF BEING

Once you have eaten of the flesh, so to speak, you must ride it out completely. You must enter the phantasmagoria of matter, and weave your way through the constant chaos before emerging out the other side into calm. You must flow as a wild river flows, crashing through endless chasms and canyons before widening out and merging with the calm, infinite sea.

This is the gauntlet which the great emptiness incarnates into so as to reveal the nature of the paradigm, and so to show the way to freedom within this realm. For it is only after living *through* it, becoming whole *within* it, and being born *out* of it, that one can know the way *beyond* it.

This is a liberation which is not an escape from this realm, but is instead an expansion of our finite dimensions into infinite depth and possibility.

To wed the great impersonal Him to the great personal Her, is to bring the space into the substance, and the substance into the space, and so to unify the great, free, transcendent spirit with the immense, essential, immanent soul.

Through this union the earthly realm becomes galactic.

What follows are brief passages describing this unity.

*

We are accomplished by the stillness which does not accomplish.

To enter the stillness is to become the Dreamer.

To become the Dreamer is to release the dream.

This is to slow down and to feel the essence of union below the pandemonium of the stormy mundane, where the surface rages on but there is calm beneath the sea.

Most action is simply flight from self.

We must remain with the tension of stillness.

'Should', 'could', and 'would' must be abandoned.

To get to the subtle presence of eternity requires an inner stillness and effortlessness which must become the operational reality of the individual

This 'intimate witness' is unaffected by all, yet permeates all.

To become this is to cross over into non-effort, and be non-being.

Either way, it remains an enigma.

*

To expand beyond the limits of this paradigm does not require understanding- for understanding is a function of the paradigm.

To expand beyond the limits of this paradigm does not require effort- for effort is a function of the paradigm.

All events in the realm of duality and time require effort. But effort cannot take us to the eternal self, because the eternal self is effortless.

What is required of us is effortless, identitiless awareness.

This is non-doing, non-thinking, non-desiring, which is Tao.

To become Tao is to become the creative fire which is alive without doing, which is to become the non-doer.

By stopping all doing the hidden Doer emerges. It can do no other.

In this way we dissolve into the all without leaving.

In this way we are liberated by not trying to be liberated.

*

Effort is gross, Non-effort is subtle
Going somewhere, one expands in one direction.
Going nowhere, one expands in every direction.
The Tao is not somewhere, the Tao is everywhere.

All things are somewhere, while nothingness is everywhere.

The Tao is the nothingness that is everywhere.

To become the nothingness that is everywhere is to become the subtle space which is found nowhere.

The subtle space cannot be found by seeking.
The subtle space cannot be known by knowing.
The subtle space cannot be accomplished by striving.
Tao is the goal which cannot be sought.

Effortlessness is the non-accomplishment which accomplishes the space.

*

To stop time is to stop effort.
Stop all effort and time ends.
The end of time *is* eternity.
Eternity does not begin nor end. It is.
Eternity is subtle. Time is gross.
Eternity has no identity. Time has names.
All that is timeless flows under, above, and through all that is of time.
Timelessness is without beginning or end.
Time changes.
Eternity is changeless.
Eternity is now.
Now *is* eternity.

*

Identity is time.
Time is identity.
To evaporate from identity is to become the subtle, eternal self that was never born, will never die, and is not bound, nor effortful, nor obstructed.
All ambition, effort, worry, and desire are bound to time and identity.
Identity is somewhere.
Non-identity is everywhere.
Identitilessness is a now that is everywhere.

To stop looking backward is to be the eternal creator of the eternal change called now.
'Now' is the embrace between being and not-being.
The membrane where the union between consciousness and being, spirit and flesh, ether and matter happens, is the eternal now orgasmic moment of our true wholeness. Newness is the birth of this never ending harmonic convergence.
To be in the newness is to be here now, and not here now. One now. Two places. One.

No time but now.
No place but here.
Eternity.
Now.

*

Eternity is the flow that is always now.
Now is the eternal flowing self which is all of existence. All of it. One flowing now Self. Now. All of it. Flowing now. Eternally.
Eternity is not profound, it is subtle.
Now is not time.
Now is the absence of time.
Everything is always new.
Now is what has never happened before.
Isness flows as the now that has never happened before.
All life is the ubiquitous, instantaneous living now-moment of Tao.
Death is the absence of the ever-flowing now.
We are eternally a radical new flowing creation.
Now, now, now, now. Always the beginning. Always now.
Now is the eternal now ever occurring now.

*

To be still is to listen to the eternity of now.
Stillness is always now.
Right here.
Right now.
Eternal, deathless, oneness, is going on now.
It *is* now.
Stillness permeates movement. The formless ensconces form. Time meets eternity in the sublime flow called now.

To get to the still point of the changeless, eternal now is to find the subtle self which never begins nor ends, but permeates all that comes and goes.
The subtle self is no self.

Eternity is a pristine stillness beyond self and other, though it includes self and other.

To go beyond the self that is born and dies is to be the self that is the stillness of no-self.

*

Can we become absent in the midst of the present?
Can we be empty, *and* doing?
Can we learn to not-exist inside existence?

It is only the ego, standing in front of the light, which casts a shadow. To be nothing and stand in the light is to illuminate all, without shadow.

To surrender shadow is to become light.

To surrender self is to become Self.

However, we can never get rid of our eternal selves. And so we surrender ourselves only so that we can be the Self; we become empty only so that we can be full; we die as a separate self, only to be born as the all.

When the great emptiness pours through us, out into form, the difference between inside and outside vanishes, because the membrane between these two has been washed away. All is one emptiness now. No inside or outside. Only one- the great, everything emptiness.

To stay in that emptiness while operating in the form, is to bring the invisible light of Self into the shadow of self.

This is to settle the emptiness into the form, and so to see through the form into the unformed.

*

The subtle witness, which we are, of the gross being, which we also are, is the crossing over and crossing back nature of our dual selves which are one.

We must watch ourselves as if we were watching another person, and also *be* ourselves intimately. That is how we pay attention to ourselves being. That is how we be *and* not-be. This is how we cross over, and cross back.

The eternal, infinite Self includes this realm, but is not limited by this realm.

We must accept *and* release, and be firm *and* soluble, so as to avoid getting caught in identity, and yet be *of* the world.

To get caught in identity is to accept limitation.

To de-identify is to expand.

We run aground when we chase after the ephemeral instead of dwelling in the everlasting.

To be aware of the everlasting Self is to be the whole.

To be whole is to be non-reactive to the particular.

*

To transcend the paradigm is to become liberated.

To identify with the paradigm is to become contained.

We must experience our Self as neither labeled nor bound, so as to be a mystery.

To be mystery is to be free.

The forces which have caused us to believe that we exist only within this paradigm have no power over lucid ignorance, because such uncontained wonder cannot be caged within by concept.

To say 'I' without knowing what 'I' is, is to begin the journey to immortality.

I is everywhere.

Therefore it has no name.

Everything is I.

Therefore there is no I.

The eternal self is the eye beyond the I, the self beyond the self, the awareness which is stillness, the stillness which is awareness.

This is the great void.

All things are contained in the void, but only no-things are one with the void.

Anything that can be said of anything cannot be said of the void.

The void is beyond everything that is, was, or will be.

This is the transcendent realm.

When one encounters the void a slight grin emerges.

This is not the void smiling, it is the reaction of the not-void knowing it is the void.

The void is not a cold nothingness, for it is beyond coldness and nothingness.

It is impersonal awareness.

*

To awaken to impersonal awareness is to be the conscious void which has no being.
That which has being is somewhere.
That which has no being is everywhere.
To attain such ubiquity is to lose location.
To be everywhere is to lose perspective.
The subtle, eternal self permeates all, is involved with all, but is beyond all, for it is everywhere.
To find our ubiquity we must go beyond all.
We must cross over before we can cross back.
To dissolve into the void is to become the formless stillness permeating all form- the great impersonal awareness beyond all knowing.
This is how we cross over.

*

To be the eternal emptiness within the ephemeral form is to transform the world with unconditioned love.
This is how we cross back.
To become aware of the eternal self is to distill the essence which is the stillness of eternity out of the movement which is ephemeral; it is to become the formless stillness which pervades all active form.
This is when all energy bonds and karma are harmonized into the quiescent, everlasting One.
This is the dispassionate ubiquity of the subtle, characterless Self.
The identitiless Self, the free one.
The nameless Tao.
The Atman.
The ocean without end.
One homeostatic, living, divisionless ubiquity.
To live without division, without walls, is to be the subtle Self of all that is.
This is to ease into the emptiness, and to slip between the cracks.

We enter the emptiness through the form.
But to truly enter the emptiness, we must *be* the emptiness.
Hollow, hole, holy, wholly, whole.
All of it.

*

To not-do amidst the doing is to enter the stillness.
This is the art of *wei wu wei*: to act without action.
To act without action is to be the stillness of nothingness inside the movement of somethingness.
To find pristine internal stillness is to fuel external stillness, for true stillness is everywhere.
This is the union of inside and out.
This union is more subtle than duality.
Duality is movement.
Oneness is still.
To be the one stillness is to end reaction.
To end reaction is to act without acting.
This is to be *in* Tao.

*

Tao is not an accomplishment, for the Tao is eternally present.
To accomplish that which cannot be accomplished is to enter what is eternally accomplished.
To accomplish this is impossible.
To not accomplish this is impossible.
All things move in and out of Tao, but the eternal Tao remains.
To remain is to continue after all else is gone.
Between all that comes and goes exists the Tao that remains.
To remain is to be eternal amidst all that comes and goes.
Tao is beyond all that comes and goes.
To see through all that comes and goes, is to see through the paradigm.
After this one can *feel* the eternal Tao that neither comes nor goes.

This is the great space that is the subtle awareness.

*

To be the great aware space permeating all that comes and goes is to *be* the eternal Tao.
To be Tao is to be liberated from all that is not Tao.
To be space is to be liberated from all that has boundaries.
To be awareness is to be liberated from the one who is aware.
This is to go beyond subject and object.
Awareness is the impersonal Tao space which is beyond all association and dimension.
Tao has no similarity.
Tao has no description.
Tao has no identity.
To be such is to be free amidst unfreedom.
This is liberation.
To be liberated is not to escape the paradigm, but to dissolve into eternal awareness.
Eternal awareness is subtle, and everywhere, so it need go nowhere.

*

Meditation is nothing more than the art of doing nothing.
Stillness is an actuality beyond doing and non-doing.
Stillness is the substratum.
The Doer is absolutely still, all else is the Doing, whether it be done through action, thought, or emotion.
To become the Doer who does not do, is to cross over.
To consciously do nothing is to master the doing.
We arrive at the *do-nothing* stage- the *wu wei*- after all the things we came to do are done, because once we have taken on the flesh, we must see it through completely; we must go the whole distance and back again.
This is to cross over and then to cross back.
We must finish with what we came to do, so that we can not-do what we came to not-do.

We must attain many things before we can attain that which cannot be attained, which is to say the Tao.

*

The eternal self is subtle.
To realize the eternal is to become dispassionate to all the gross waves of the manifest.
This is to allow the paradigm to wash over and through us, so as to maintain awareness of our subtle existence.
It is when we are addicted to anything created that we are also addicted to being created. It is only when we stop being addicted to being created that we become the stillness of the Creator.
Identity is our greatest addiction.
Pride will entangle us in identity.
Shame will entangle us in identity.
Fear will entangle us in identity.
And so will courage.
Any reaction to the paradigm is *of* the paradigm.
Action must arise out of the eternal void, the Tao, the identitiless stillness which exists prior to manifestation, in order for it not to be entangled.
Liberation is awakening to the ever-free identitiless presence permeating the confined, gross form.
This is to set the confined form free.

*

The unmoving yet living center from which we witness the true dynamic nature of created being is a place of receptive surrender, of complete concavity; this is the vacuum, the total absence, the void into which all that is not void is drawn, destroyed, and reborn.
The wheel revolves around the hub.
The hub is motionless absence.
The center which is the hub, is nowhere until it is found within. Then it is everywhere.

To transcend the paradigm is not to rise above it, but to fall away behind it, and then to explode throughout it.

To fall away is to not care.
To explode throughout it is to care.
To be the stillness permeating the all is to care without caring, and to give without giving.
This is the empty benediction of the Tao.

*

In the stillness which does not accomplish all is accomplished eternally.
To distill the eternal stillness out of the gross movement is to cross over.
To become the eternal stillness in the gross movement is to cross back.
To cross back is to express immortality into mortality.
This is to become a 'piercing through' of the temporal, with the laser sharpness of Buddha-mind.
This is to penetrate all happenings cleanly, seamlessly, and be free from the all while being the all.

.

*

The eternal, non-being Self is distilled out of the form, and then it returns to permeate all form.
The witness and witnessed are thus integrated. All juxtaposition has ended. We have infiltrated the entire breadth of the cosmos, intertwining our subtle strands into the glorious fabric of being.
Oceanic consciousness united with earthly soul.
Mixed within, poured without.
To be the eternal absence in the midst of the temporal presence is to be the Great Consciousness united with the Great Being.
This is to be one with the Father and Mother, with God and Goddess, with Heaven and Earth.
When emptiness is distilled out of the form, Big Mind emerges as the space within which all being exists. That space is then re-integrated into isness.
We are the re-integrators of the great emptiness of God, with the deep soul of Goddess.

We are both.
As we dissolve, they become one.
This is cosmic androgyny.

To always be able to find and feel the cold, clean emptiness within the hot, throbbing form, is to be united with God and Goddess.

This is to act in the whirling cacophony of the kaleidoscopic emanations, while yet dancing unmovingly in the eternity of the motionless One.

To identify with the formless eternity is to become a self-substantial entirety.

To identify with the manifest form is to actualize your present emanation.

Two identities, one Self.
This is wholeness.

*

Wholeness operates differently than duality.
Wholeness is impartial, duality is in parts.
Wholeness is two that are one.
Duality is one that is two.
Oneness knows no other, no distance, no division.
Duality knows no mystery.
Tao is the subtle mysterious oneness beyond division.
It is in and through everything, but it is no-thing.
To enter this space we must *become* space.
To become space is to become all space.
To become all space is to embrace all form.
To embrace all form is to know no division.
This is universal love.
This is the redemption of the world.

*"Empowered to penetrate others
With primordial waves of bliss,
Shimmering resonant love webs
Spread out to boundlessness."*
Alex Grey[76]

---

[76] *Transfigurations*, p119. Inner Traditions, USA. 2001

Books by Jack Haas

In and Of: *memoirs of a mystic journey*
ISBN: 0-9731007-1-0

Roots and Wings: *adventures of a spirit on earth*
ISBN: 0-9731007-4-5

OM, baby! *a pilgrimage to the eternal self*
ISBN: 0-9734677-1-1

The Way of Wonder: *a return to the mystery of ourselves*
ISBN: 0-9731007-0-2

The Dream of Being: *aphorisms, ideograms, and aislings*
ISBN: 0-9731007-5-3

HER: *the sacred naked mother earth, and the divine feminine soul*
ISBN: 0-9734677-7-0

www.ingramcontent.com/pod-product-compliance
Lightning Source LLC
Chambersburg PA
CBHW032121090426
42743CB00007B/418